SIMONSBATH
THE INSIDE STORY OF AN EXMOOR VILLAGE

SIMONSBATH
THE INSIDE STORY OF AN EXMOOR VILLAGE

by

ROGER A. BURTON

Author of *THE HERITAGE OF EXMOOR*

R.A.B. 1994

Researched, written and published
by
ROGER A. BURTON

Direct sales and all enquiries to
12 Style Close
Rumsam
Barnstaple
N. Devon EX32 9EL

Tel: 0271 78491

Printed by Maslands Ltd., 16a Fore Street, Tiverton, Devon

CONTENTS

TO MAG
of Rose Cottage, Simonsbath

LIST OF ILLUSTRATIONS

Dust Jacket - from a painting by Ian Hudson.

Frontispiece - Frederic Knight. *Courtesy of the Committee of the Allerford Rural Life Museum.*

ACKNOWLEDGEMENTS

A history such as this could not have been written without the help of many people. It is my pleasant duty here to thank all who have helped to make this book possible.

Firstly I would like to express my thanks and appreciation to the archivists and staff of the Devon Record Office and West Country Studies Library in Exeter, the Somerset Record Office and West Country History Library in Taunton; the Reference Section of Kidderminster Library, Worcestershire, and the North Devon Record Office and Local Studies Library in my home town of Barnstaple for all the courteous help I have received over a period of many years.

I would now like to thank Lady Margaret Fortescue of Castle Hill, Filleigh, and Mr Hugh Thomas, the Fortescue Estate's Agent for their continued support and for generously allowing access to documents and other records not normally available to the general public, also Margaret Pine who is employed in the Estate Office, for her help in locating some of the items I was searching for.

My grateful thanks too are due to a very dear friend, Margaret (Mag) Prout, for her help in sorting out Simonsbath families and for providing much other useful information, even though she refuses to let me publish some of it. I would also like to pay tribute to the late Jack Buckingham who lived with Harry and Mag at Rose Cottage for many years. While researching this book I found myself constantly referring to notes taken during the last few years of his life.

Others who have provided useful material include Anne Buckingham and Dorothy (Dor) Little, both of whom are now living in North Molton, but formerly of Simonsbath and Exmoor; also Stan and Millie Curtis, Sante Lafuente, and Brian Duke of Simonsbath; Frank and Olive Vigars of Bossington—formerly of Simonsbath and Honeymead; and the Rev. Atkins, former Vicar of Exmoor, for making available the parish registers not held in the Somerset Record Office; and anyone else who has helped in any way.

My thanks too, to all who have contributed photographs (see under list of illustrations), also to my sister Eileen Dolling for her work on the maps and plans in this book, and my typists, Kathleen Margaret Lewis, who unfortunately broke her arm just as she was on the point of typing up the last two chapters, and Fran Dean who kindly stepped in and finished the job.

Finally I would like to thank Ian Hudson for the fine dust jacket, and Chris May, Andy Jackson and all the staff at Maslands, Tiverton for the fine team work that has gone into preparing and printing this book. It has been a real pleasure working with them.

Roger Alan Burton
Barnstaple 1994

9

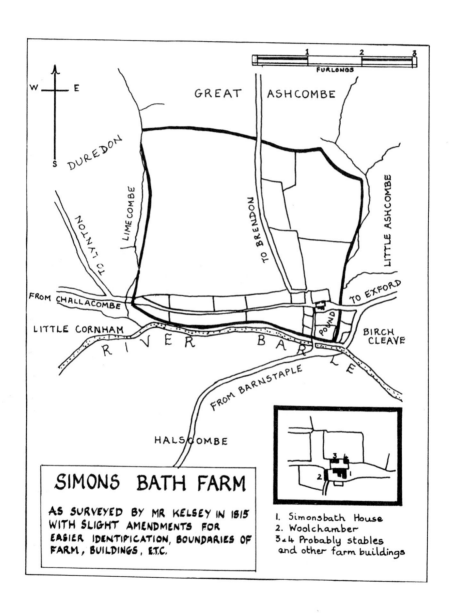

FURLONGS

W E
S

GREAT ASHCOMBE

DUREDON

LIMECOMBE

TO LYNTON

TO BRENDON

LITTLE ASHCOMBE

FROM CHALLACOMBE

TO EXFORD

LITTLE CORNHAM

POND

BIRCH CLEAVE

RIVER BARLE

FROM BARNSTAPLE

HALSCOMBE

3 4
2 1

SIMONS BATH FARM

AS SURVEYED BY MR KELSEY IN 1815
WITH SLIGHT AMENDMENTS FOR
EASIER IDENTIFICATION, BOUNDARIES OF
FARM, BUILDINGS, E.T.C.

1. Simonsbath House
2. Woolchamber
3 & 4 Probably stables
and other farm buildings

FOREWORD

CASUAL visitors to the lovely Exmoor village of Simonsbath can be forgiven for assuming that the near perfect balance of luxuriant trees and fine pastures around it, with the river and open moorland beyond, was always so, but in reality, much of the beauty in the eye of the beholder has been wrought by the hand of man and that only within the last 175 years.

The village lies at a height of about 1050 feet above sea level and is situated at the very heart of what was once the Royal Forest of Exmoor, now the parish of Exmoor, but more usually referred to as Exmoor Proper.

Although Exmoor is by far the largest parish in Somerset, it has to some extent lost its identity since the creation of the National Park of Exmoor in 1952, of which it is but a small though still a very significant part.

By comparison with other moorland villages within the National Park, Simonsbath is a modern village, with only one house—built in 1654—predating the Inclosure of the Royal Forest in 1818, when, after Parliament, on behalf of the Crown, sold the largest part of the Forest to John Knight—an ironmaster from Worcestershire—the foundations of the village we see today were laid down and trees planted around it for shelter, and to enhance the beauty of this lonely spot.

Because Simonsbath is of comparatively recent date it has been possible to trace its history, and that of most of its inhabitants, with a greater degree of accuracy than is normally possible. There will, of course, always be many gaps in our knowledge; a situation that has not been helped by the Census Returns for Exmoor, where we find most of the dwelling houses in the village listed under the common heading of Simonsbath, making it difficult in some instances to identify where some of the people listed, actually lived. Nevertheless, persistent research in all the channels open to me has paid off, and many hitherto unanswered questions have, I believe, now been satisfactorily resolved.

I apologise here and now to readers of my first book if one or two of the stories told herein have a familiar ring to them, but it has been found necessary to include them in order to provide continuity and a balanced account. Please bear with me, and as the story of Simonsbath and its inhabitants unfolds, I feel sure, that you will be surprised at some of the turn of events. In many ways it is an unusual story, and quite possibly one that is unique in the annals of English history.

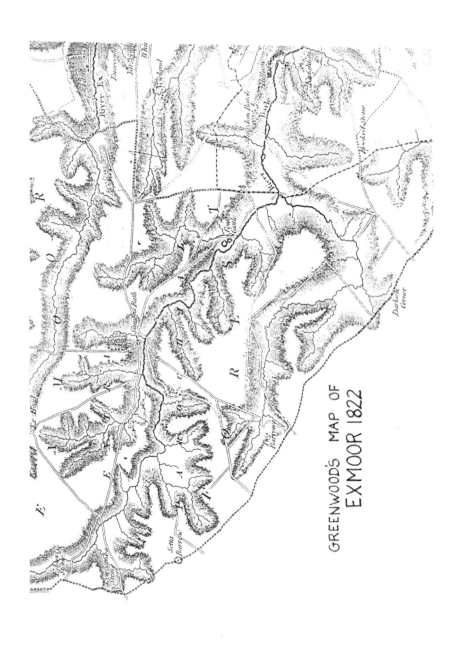

GREENWOOD'S MAP OF
EXMOOR 1822

CHAPTER 1

THE HISTORICAL BACKGROUND

THE earliest description we have of Simonsbath is that recorded by John Leland a century before the first house was built there. Leland, who had been appointed by Henry VIII to travel the length and breadth of England to search out and record its antiquities, passed this way in 1540 on a journey from Dunster to Barnstaple. He describes this part of his travels as follows:

"From Exford to Simonsbath Bridge a 4 miles al by Forest, Baren and Morisch Ground, wher ys store and breeding of yong Catelle, but little or no Corne or Habitation.

There rennith at this Place caullid Simonsbath a Ryver betwixt to great Morisch Hilles in a depe Botom, and ther is a Bridge of Woode over this Water.

The Water in Somer most communely rennith flat apon stones easy to be passid over, but when Raynes cum and Stormes of Wyntre it Ragith and ys depe.

Always this Streame ys a great deale bygger Water than Ex is at Exford, yet it resortith into Ex Ryver.

The Boundes of Somersetshire go beyond this streame one way by North West (should be South West) a 2 miles or more to a place caullid the Spanne and the Tourres; for there be Hillokkes of Yerth cast up in anncient tyme for Markes and Limites betwixt Somersetshir and Devonshir, and here about is the Limes and Boundes of Exmore forest.

From Simonsbath Bridge I rode up a high Morisch Hylle and so passing by 2 myles in lyke ground, the soyle began to be sumwhat fruteful, and the Hilles to be ful of Enclosures, ontylle I cam a 3 miles farther to a poor Village caullid Brayforde, wher rennith a Broke by likelihood resorting to Simonsbath Water and Ex."

In Leland's day Simonsbath was little more than a name on a map—if there was one; a meeting place of old rough tracks converging at the centre of the ancient Royal Forest of Exmoor, with a footbridge over the River Barle; a bridge that was in a state of great decay in 1652, for want of repair. This bridge, long gone, was situated about 100 yards downstream of the present bridge, at the spot where the old road crossed the river.

There are a number of traditions as to how Simonsbath got its name. One is that a deep pool—upstream of the bridge—was the bathing place of an outlaw named Simon, once the scourge of Exmoor, but it is not known when or where he lived. Another tradition connects the pool with King Sigmund, the dragon slayer.

Yet another suggestion, and one that appears to be more logical, is that Simonsbath is a corruption of Simons Path, which, it is reasonable to assume, crossed the River Barle at this point; the Simon in this instance being Siegmund the legendary Danish leader and hero, who, tradition has it, aided the Celtic tribes in the Exmoor Region in their resistance against the Saxons after being cast ashore on the Exmoor Coast.

As far as written evidence is concerned the earliest reference to Simonsbath appears to be that recorded in Leylands Itinerary.

In the aftermath of the Civil War, which had culminated with the execution of Charles I in 1649, an Act of Parliament was passed to dispose of all the royal properties and estates. Shortly after, a survey of the Royal Forest of Exmoor took place, followed in 1652 by the sale of it to a Joseph Strange, who proved to be no more than the front man for the real purchasers, James Boevey and John Smith, who acquired the whole of the Forest, which at this time extended to just over 20,000 acres, for the sum of £12,329.5.5., which after allowances had been made in respect of the existing leaseholder; and the owner of the tithes, reduced the figure Parliament finally received to £6,851.14.6. By the time the final settlement had been reached, Boevey had acquired the tithe rights.

Although this book is essentially a history of the village of Simonsbath, it is necessary here to give a brief account of the Forest and the way in which it was administered, in order to avoid any confusion later.

First it should be made clear that the Royal Forest of Exmoor was not a forest in its true sense, but had since time immemorial been a summer pasturing ground, mainly for sheep—about 40,000 a year at this time, along with about 1,000 head of cattle and 500 horses—mostly Exmoor ponies. About two thirds of the sheep came from the moorland parishes bordering on to the Forest; the remainder from parishes further afield. The profit to the Warden—or Lessee—of the Forest was upward of £350 a year after all expenses had been paid—a considerable sum in those days.

The day-to-day running of the Forest and the collection of pasturage dues was left to a Deputy Forester. Certain other duties were carried out by two large bodies of men, namely the Free Suitors of the 52 ancient tenements that made up the parishes of Hawkridge and Withypool; and the Suitors at Large from the other parishes bordering the Forest.

Both the Free Suitors and Suitors at Large were expected to attend the two Forest Courts held each year; the first at Lanacre; the second a fortnight later at Hawkridge. The Free Suitors were also responsible for driving the Forest nine times a year on horseback; five times for horses; twice, sometimes three times for cattle, and once for sheep. The drive for sheep took place nine days before midsummer, by which time all sheep pasturing in the Forest should have been returned to their home farms for shearing, after which they were driven back to the Forest to finish the grazing season. Any sheep left behind were driven to the Forest Pound at Withypool and shorn, with the fleece going to the Warden of the Forest, and the sheep also if not claimed by Midsummer Day. All animals found trespassing on the Forest were also impounded until a fine was paid.

The Free Suitors were also expected to perambulate the Forest Bounds once every seven years and to serve on a Coroners Inquest should any corpse be found within the Forest. In return for these services each of the Free Suitors was entitled to free pasturage for 140 sheep on the Forest, and the same for five mares and their foals, and as many cattle as could be wintered on their tenements plus other privileges which included all the peat, heath and fern they could use on their farms in the winter, and certain rights of fishing on the rivers of the Forest.

The main duties of the Suitors at Large—apart from attending the Forest Courts—appear to have been the maintenance of the boundary stones and other marks which separated their own commons from the Forest, and to keep the Forest free of trespassers. For these minor duties and a small quit rent they were entitled to pasture their sheep, horses and cattle on Exmoor at half the rates paid by outsiders.

Thus things stood when James Boevey and John Smith acquired the Freehold of the Forest of Exmoor in 1652. The Forest was then divided between the partners with Smith taking the greater share, namely the land south of the Exford-Challacombe road. It is apparent that he was only interested in obtaining a good return on his investment. Boevey, on the other hand, appears to have had a real hankering for the country life after years of indifferent health while making a fortune in the City of London, where for some years past he had been in business as a merchant. To this end, he built a fine house at Simonsbath—now the Simonsbath House Hotel—and around it enclosed 108 acres of the moorland for a farm. He also built a new pound at Simonsbath, in the river meadow in front of his house to replace the centuries old pound at Withypool, although the latter did remain in use for many years thereafter.

On the completion of his new house in 1654, Boevey and his second wife, Isobel, took up residence there. No doubt the solitude of the place acted as a stimulus to his ever active mind for it was here that he is believed to have written many of the 32 books—mostly philosophical—accredited to him.

In the same year that James Boevey took up residence in Simonsbath, he leased John Smith's portion of the Forest for a term of 2000 years at a fixed annual rent of £130, and thus gained control of all of the Forest.

All went well until 1660 when the Monarchy was restored, and with it all the Crown property disposed of by Parliament. This meant that Boevey and Smith no longer owned the Forest. Moreover they forfeited the money they had paid for it, but Boevey, a born schemer if ever there was one, had forseen this possibility and had purchased the remaining term of the last life lease of the Forest and thus became sole lessee and tithe owner of the Forest of Exmoor. His next step was to extend the life of his lease and this he succeeded in doing with the purchase of a new lease for a term of three lives plus 31 years.

One of the first changes made by James Boevey on gaining possession of the Forest had been to double the rates for stock pasturing there, but he was quickly forced to reduce them again when farmers responded by sending less sheep to graze on Exmoor, and by moving their sheep on and off the Forest at night and various other schemes, sought to avoid the payment of their dues. When Boevey got wind of what was going on, he took the offending farmers to Court to recover the monies owed him, and so began a succession of law suits that was to keep him busy for the next 40 years.

In 1675, Boevey laid claim to the commons of all the parishes bordering the Forest, on the grounds that as they were once part of the Royal Forest— of which he was the Lessee—they were his by right; a claim which had it been successful would have entitled him to the tithes of all the sheep pasturing thereon, thus greatly increasing his income, at the expense of the parsons of the parishes concerned, who were accustomed to receiving these tithes. Fortunately, Boevey did not succeed with his claims, for which the parsons must have been exceedingly thankful.

The number of people living in the one house at Simonsbath at this time is, perhaps, surprising. Besides Boevey—now a widower—there was Edward Burt, husbandman, who had lived there for the past 25 years; Richard Crosswell, Yeoman, age 27 and Henry Smith aged about 30, who was Boevey's Deputy Forester. All appeared as witnesses during the court hearings in respect of Boevey's claims for the Commons. Whether or not any of them were married is not known, but if not, there were probably one or two domestic servants also living in the house.

In or about the year 1680, James Boevey married for the third time. Shortly after, he and his new wife left Exmoor and retired to Cheam in Surrey, leaving the day-to-day running of the Forest in the capable hands of his Deputy Forester, Henry Smith. Henry was still around in 1694, when, with the help of a Richard Crang, he made an inventory of the contents of Simonsbath House and Farm, following the death of the first known tenant there, Richard Hill. This historic document, held in the Somerset Record Office at Taunton, has already been set down in my first book, but because it is so very much a part of the history of Simonsbath it is also recorded here, as follows:

Simons—Burrow Inventory
Richard Hill

An inventory of the goods of Richard Hill of Simons-Bath lately deceased, taken and priced the 18th day of April, 1694, by Henry Smith and Richard Crang as followeth

		£.	s.	d.
Item	his wearing apparell	2.	0.	0.
"	two cows and calves	9.	0.	0.
"	four yearlings	5.	0.	0.
"	three pigs	2.	0.	0.
"	one old .o..(boar? pony?) could be anything	0.	5.	0.
"	three score ewes...r (poor?) lean sheep	20.	10.	0.
"	Poultry	0.	5.	0.
"	two table boards and three formes	0.	15.	0.
"	three ... stools	0.	2.	0.
"	one cubbord	0.	10.	0.

		£. s. d.
Item four pewter dishes, two plates, a candlestick and a salt		0. 10. 0
" two brass pans and a kettle		1. 6. 0.
" three brass pots and a skillet		1. 1. 6.
" two brewing vates, three tubs, four screens? and three little vessells		0. 16. 0.
" an old cheese press and four cheese vates (vats)		0. 4. 0.
" six flagons		0. 6. 0.
" two feather beds, bolsters, coverletts and blankets belonging to them		7. 10. 0.
" two other beds with coverlets and blankets to them		1. 13. 4.
" three pairs of old sheets, two table cloths and six table napkins		1. 0. 4.
" three bedsteads ... chest and two coffers		1. 7. 4.
" Andirons, pot hooks and pot hangings		0. 2. 0.
" two pack saddles, a hackney saddle, girls and a rooks		0. 4. 6.
" two brandices, a fender and two spits		0. 5. 0.
" an old gun, a yoke, bows and a seale		0. 6. 6.
" a trundle salter and vates (vats)		0. 18. 6.
" other small tools and things out of mind and unseen		0. 3. 4.
		£56. 1. 10.

N.B. Although the valuation was probably an accurate
assessment of the value of the estate, the arithmetic
leaves a little to be desired and the total should, I think, be   £58. 1. 4.

Certain items in the inventory, such as the table cloths, table napkins and
sheets, indicate that Richard Hill was not of ordinary farming stock, but
what we would now call a gentleman farmer, and from the number of
brewing items listed it would appear that he supplemented his income by the
sale of ale, or beer. There was certainly some demand for this commodity,
because we know from later accounts that the yearly cutting (castrating) of
colts at Simonsbath, was always followed by an allowance of beer for the
men assisting with this hard and thirsty work. Beer was also provided when
a survey (sale) of colts took place, and the Deputy Forester usually managed
to justify its consumption on other occasions as well. There would also have
been a limited passing trade, comprised of packhorse train drivers, drovers
and stockmen going about their duties, and so, although Simonsbath House
was not licensed as an inn until 1789 this was merely giving some legality to
a practice that had been carried out regularly over a period of some 100 years
prior to obtaining the licence.

James Boevey died at Cheam in 1696. He had held the Forest for 43 years,
the longest time that any one man had held it in its lengthy history as a Royal
Forest. After his death, his widow retained it for a further eight years before
selling the remaining 15 years of her lease to Robert Siderfin of Croydon
House, Timberscombe, who took over the Forest in 1704, and was fortunate
in obtaining a further lease, giving him possession to 1750.

Neither Robert Siderfin nor any of his sucessors as lease-holders and Wardens of the Forest ever lived in Simonsbath House. For the most part thereafter it was the customary home of the Deputy Forester, who was usually also the tenant of the farm. In 1702, however, two years before Robert Siderfin gained possession of the Forest, William Smith—Henry Smith's successor as Agent or Deputy Forester to Madam Boevey—had let Simonsbath Farm to John Dennicombe for the very modest rental of £9 p.a.; the loneliness of the situation no doubt having some bearing on the rent. Dennicombe was granted a new lease by Siderfin, for a term of five years, subject to a full repairing agreement, for which a bond for £500 was deposited with his landlord as security. Towards the end of the five years, with nothing having been done by way of repairs, the premises were in a ruinous state and Dennicombe was given notice to put the place in order. He pleaded with Robert Siderfin that he could not afford the repairs, but if his landlord would do them, he promised to repay him. The repairs were done, and Dennicombe was allowed to stay on as yearly tenant after his five years were up, but in 1717 he was given notice to quit.

In 1718, Dennicombe's wife pleaded with Siderfin for permission to remain in part of the house until midsummer. This was agreed, but when the time came, Dennicombe refused to go and he was then arrested and taken to Ilchester Gaol—the usual treatment for debtors. Robert Siderfin then brought an action at the Winter Assizes for ejectment. Judgement was given in his favour, and on the 22nd of April 1718 the rest of the Dennicombe family were turned out on the Moor.

Four days after the ejectment a suit in Chancery began, with Dennicombe claiming that Siderfin had no right to throw him out as he had laid out large sums of money in the last year on improvements and manure for the farm. This was disputed by Siderfin who said he doubted 5/- had ever been spent on the farm by his tenant. Moreover, Dennicombe had burnt just about all the timber, doors, etc., in the house and buildings for fuel. No record of the outcome of the case has been found but it seems most unlikely that Dennicombe stood any chance of winning his case, or for that matter his freedom for some time.

Very little of importance concerning Simonsbath in the next 40 years or so has been discovered. Forest Account Books in the Acland Archive in the Devon Record Office at Exeter covering this period make no mention of the one house and small farm, nor who was in residence there.

A diligent search of the church registers of all the parishes bordering onto—or close to—the Forest of Exmoor has yielded only one name in regards to Simonsbath for the period in question. This was found in the Porlock registers, when on the 23rd April, 1739, Thomas Comer of Bratton Fleming married Sarah Strong of Simonsbath, but whether she was the daughter of an occupant there, or just a servant girl, is not known.

In 1767, Sir Thomas Acland of Holnicote obtained a lease of the Forest, and shortly after carried out major renovations to the old house at Simonsbath at a cost of £203. 3. 2½, which included new timber to the value of £60, which suggests that little—if any—money had been spent on repairs for a long time. Two years later a further £52. 16. 9½, was expended on the property, £25. 12. 5. of which went to pay a mason and £16. 1. 10½, to a carpenter; the remainder for materials used.

Nothing has been found to suggest that John Hill of Withypool—who was the Deputy Forester at the time Sir T. D. Acland took possession of the Forest—ever lived at Simonsbath*. The same can be said of his successor John Zeal, who held office for two years, 1768 and 69, but we do know that Amos Hole, who was the Deputy Forester in 1770 and part of 1771, lived at Simonsbath, because that was the address given when his son William was baptised at Exford Church in July 1771. We know too from our search of Parish Registers around the Moor that they were not the first members of the Hole family to live at Simonsbath. The Bratton Fleming registers record the baptism of William, the son of Richard and Jane Hole of Simonsbath in March 1758, and in December of the same year, Joan Hole of Simonsbath was married to David Rawle, yeoman of Challacombe, at the latter Church.

By the time William Hole was baptised at Exford in 1771, his father, Amos—Deputy Forester and tenant of Simonsbath Farm—had been dead for two months. He was buried at North Molton. His widow, Ann, was still living at the farm when she married Henry Smyth at North Molton in October 1772, and the parish registers record that the couple were still at Simonsbath when their son Henry was baptised in the following year.

The next Deputy Forester and tenant of Simonsbath Farm was Richard Court—the rent for the farm at this time being £35 a year, including tithes of £7. Richard died in 1779 and was buried at Exford—the parish registers describing him as 'of Simonsbath'. At the time of his death the duties of Deputy Forester were shared between Robert and Thomas Court, and probably the farm as well, though Robert was the tenant. For the first three years of his tenancy he paid an increased rental of £40 a year, but must have been hard pressed to meet the increased rent charge and in 1780, the year before his death, the rent was reduced to £35, and remained at that figure until the Royal Forest of Exmoor was disafforested in 1818.

In his 'History of the Forest of Exmoor', MacDermot gives William Lock as the next and last Deputy Forester of Exmoor; his term of office lasting from 1782-1819. He too was the tenant of Simonsbath Farm, and, like his predecessors, appears to have shared the one and only house there with others.

Towards the end of the 18th C, a number of changes were made in the way Exmoor affairs were conducted, putting Simonsbath more firmly on the map. Pony sales from the herd of Exmoor ponies that Sir T. D. Acland had been building up were begun in 1772. At the first sale an undisclosed number of ponies were sold for £32. 2. 0. In the following year 36 ponies were sold for £73. 9. 6., giving an average of just over £2 apiece. Further sales took place in 1777 and 79 and from that time on became more or less an annual event, with just the occasional year left out.

* His ancestor John Hill, Deputy Forester 1654-74 was resident for a time; Simonsbath being his address when he acquired a 99 year lease for Newlands, Withypool 20-7-1757.

The first of several advertisements concerning sales from the Acland herd of ponies appeared in the Exeter Flying Post on the 5th July 1788, which reads as follows: "The sale of Exmoor Horses will be held at Simonsbath House within the Forest of Exmoor on Wedneday 23rd July instant by 10 o'clock in the Forenoon, and the sale will in future be held annually on that day, unless it should fall on a Saturday or Sunday. By the particular order of Sir Thomas Dyke Acland, Bart.—Sharland, Steward of the Forest, South Molton."

A similar advertisement was placed in the same paper in the following year, with this addition. "It is expected that none of the 52 Free Suitors of the said Forest, nor any other person or persons offer any ponies for sale at Simonsbath on that day". A timely warning no doubt that Sir Thomas Acland had no intention of allowing others to take advantage of his pony sales to feather their own nests. There was no need to repeat the warning.

By the time the pony sale of 1793 was held at Simonsbath, the quality of the Exmoor ponies had been much improved. The advertisement of that year included the comment "There will be a show of fine handsome young colts and many will pair well".

In the following year the Exmoor ponies were described as being "the purest and most handsome yet bred on the Forest", but the weather was so bad on the day of the sale it was postponed. The ponies were sold later at an auction held at Higher Combe, in the parish of Dulverton, two miles from the town.

Apart from the pony sale of 1794, the venue of all of the sales advertised in the Exeter Flying Post was Simonsbath House; not Stoney Plot, where at a later date Frederic Knight was to hold his pony sales*; where to add to this rural attraction—according to a correspondent of the North Devon Journal—organised wrestling bouts were an added incentive to draw the crowds.

At some time during the latter part of the 18th C Simonsbath became the venue for the annual Forest Courts, which since time immemorial had been held at Lanacre and Hawkridge; the latter always adjourning to Withypool in the afternoon for refreshments, and this may well have been one of the reasons why Simonsbath House was officially licensed as an inn in 1789, although as we have already seen there is no reason to believe there was ever a shortage of ale there in earlier times.

According to Henry Hall Dixon (The Druid) writing in 1862 of events some 70 years earlier, there were then only five men, a woman and a little girl living on Exmoor. Dixon's informant told him that his mother was that little girl; she drew the beer at the Simonsbath Public House; a rough lot of customers they were too. Dixon goes on to relate that "the inn was also at one time much frequented by smuggling gangs, working presumably from Lynton". A logical assumption, although we do not know if he was referring to the time when John Hooper was the landlord of the inn (1797-1819). He certainly had family connections in the Lynton area. Incidentally he was

---

* Held there until 1856 when a church was built on this site.

probably living in Simonsbath much earlier than the Ale House Returns suggest, and is believed to be the John Hooper responsible for cutting (castrating) the Exmoor colts—55 in 1782.

John Hooper is also believed to have sub-leased the farm at Simonsbath and was certainly involved in the day-to-day running of the Forest. It is his name that appears in the earliest Land Tax Returns, paying the customary £83. 6. 0. for the whole of the Forest on behalf of Sir Thomas Acland.

It was probably during this period in its history that Simonsbath House became known locally as the "Baby Farm" on account of the number of wayward girls who turned up there to have their illegitimate babies. The earliest of whom we have record—discovered in the Brendon registers—is the baptism of John Jewell, son of Mary of Simonsbath, in 1791. Others followed; two in one year—1810—from Exford. William the base child of Mary Seage, and Elizabeth, base child of Mary Pugsley.

Not all of the children born at Simonsbath during this period were illegitimate. Some, like the children born to the Hole family have already been recorded, and for the sake of posterity one more, Elizabeth, the daughter of John and Mary Rudd of Simonsbath, who was baptised at Brendon in 1786, is added to the list.

Sir Thomas Dyke Acland—the first of that name—Lessee and Warden of the Forest since 1767, died in 1785. He was succeeded by Sir T. D. Acland II, who was affectionately known as 'His Honour'. He was taken ill on a journey to London in 1794, and died there soon after. Shortly before his death Sir Thomas acquired two further leases of the Forest of Exmoor, extending his term of office to 1814, but by the time his son and heir—also Sir Thomas—came of age in 1808, only six years of unexpired leases remained, and though he tried hard to obtain a further lease, Parliament, on behalf of the Crown, was considering other ways in which to increase the revenue it received from the Forest, and a further lease was denied him.

In the meantime the population of England had been growing rapidly, and with its normal supply of foreign grain cut off as a result of the Napoleonic Wars, Parliament recommended to the King (Farmer George) that a Board of Agriculture and Internal Improvement be set up to survey every county in the land to see what measures should be taken to increase the production of home grown food. John Billingsley, an eminent agriculturalist and improver in his own right, was given the task of surveying the County of Somerset, to see what could be done to improve production. His survey, of course, included the Forest of Exmoor.

Billingsley's recommendations concerning Exmoor was "that a small town or village should be established near Simonsbath House, which would form proper residences for artificers and husbandmen, to be employed in building farmhouses and inclosing a comfortable estate around them. Once a village was established it should not be difficult to get a baker, butcher and shopkeeper to settle there."

Although no heed was paid to Billingsley's suggestions at that time, there can be little doubt that his report was taken into consideration following

Parliament's decision to refuse Sir Thomas Acland's application for a new lease for the Forest while it made up its mind on its future. To this end, surveyors were sent to Exmoor to see if the land was suitable for growing oak woods to supply timber to the Navy. In the final analysis this was decided against, and the Forest was then divided into allotments to compensate all the different factions with rights thereon, with the Crown taking the largest allotment, some 10,262 acres in extent—just over half the Forest— around Simonsbath which was then put up for sale in 1818 to the highest tender. John Knight, a wealthy ironmaster from Worcestershire was the purchaser of the Crown Allotment at a cost of £50,000. He also acquired Simonsbath House and Farm—a separate lot—for £1,200.

Still hungry for land John Knight then set about buying up as many allotments on Exmoor as the new owners were prepared to sell, ending up with just over 16,000 acres, or about four-fifths of the Forest. He also purchased the adjoining manor of Brendon, which amounted to nearly 5,500 acres, including a number of useful farms.

Although the Crown Allotment and Simonsbath House and farm were not conveyed to John Knight until the 15th March 1820, he did in fact assume effective control from the day he put down his deposit in August 1818.

An advertisement in the Taunton Courier (27.8.1818) reveals that for the present he intended to continue the age-old custom of taking in sheep for summer pasturing on the Royal Allotment, albeit at greatly increased rates. Two months later, in the same paper, he issued a warning to poachers of his game and fish, and those cutting turf or heath on his property, or committing any other kind of trespass, that they would be prosecuted and punished as the law directs. Both the advertisement and the warning were signed John Knight of Simonsbath, but by the time a similar warning was issued in the following year in regards to his Brendon Estate, he was residing at Lynton and it was not until around 1830 that he again took up residence in Boeveys old house at Simonsbath.

John Knight and his son Frederic's efforts to reclaim and improve their Exmoor Estate was first told in The Reclamation of Exmoor Forest by C. S. Orwin in 1929. This book was updated by R. J. Sellick in 1970 and expanded upon in my own book The Heritage of Exmoor 1989. Very briefly, the reclamation began with the inclosure of the estate with a wall some 29 miles long; subdivided into large allotments where the moorland was too rough for easy reclamation, and into fields of 50 acres or so where it was more suitable for cultivation. Lime was hauled from kilns as far away as Combe Martin to sweeten the acid Exmoor soil, without which crops could not be grown. Fine roads were made across the Moor, Pinkworthy Pond and canal, and a similar canal off the River Exe, were constructed to provide water power to work steep inclines at both ends of a proposed railway from Porlock Weir to Simonsbath, to bring in vast quantities of cheaper limerock from South Wales to speed up the reclamation work, but for reasons explained in The Heritage of Exmoor, the railway project was never completed. The same can be said about one or two other of John Knight's more ambitious schemes.

John Knight's efforts to grow wheat in an inhospitable climate, 1,000 ft and more above sea level also came to nought, though his introduction of alien breeds of sheep and cattle from other parts of the country did meet with some success.

Changes in policy after Frederic Knight took over the management of the Exmoor Estate in 1841 led to the creation of a number of farms for letting in the traditional landlord and tenant farmer relationships, but only one or two of the early tenants—who for the most part were from outside the area and ill equipped to take on the challenge of creating a farm out of virgin moorland—succeeded in making a go of it, and later, when it became impossible to let some of these farms, they became the base for large sheepherdings, stocked with Cheviot and Blackface sheep brought down from Scotland, and shepherded by Scottish shepherds who had accompanied them down and chose to settle on the Moor.

Frederic Knight's efforts to find large deposits of iron ore on his land and the story of the mining companies who sought to wrest it from the reluctant hills has also been told in some detail in my first book. At the heart of it all the village of Simonsbath was created.

CHAPTER 2

THE BIRTH OF THE VILLAGE

BY A strange coincidence two of the first men recorded as living in Simonsbath after John Knight took possession of his estate in 1820, bore the same name—Thomas Timmins. One was described as 'of Simonsbath', farmer, when his daughter was baptised at Lynton in June 1821, and a son in 1823. His wife was called Elizabeth, and as there was only the one farm at this time, they presumably—like their predecessors before them—lived in Simonsbath House.

It is not in the Lynton parish registers that the second Thomas Timmins is to be found, but Exford, which records the baptism of a son Thomas in 1822, and daughters in 1824 and 1826, all born at Simonsbath, their father's occupation, Land Surveyor. Sadly the registers also record the untimely death of Thomas Timmins's wife Mary, at the age of only 33. Her memorial stone stands near the main path into Exford Church and reads:

> Sacred to the memory of Mary Timmins, a native of
> Sedgely, Staffordshire and wife of Thomas Timmins, who
> died at Simonsbath 24th June 1828, age 33.
>> Husband and children weep not for me I pray
>> Death calls me now I can no longer stay
>> A sudden illness did my body seize
>> Neither Human skill nor Medicine could ease
>> Til God surveyed my tenderness with woe
>> and with soft compassion gave the blow
>> Farewell my Husband and Children dear
>> It pleases the Lord to call me here
>> I trust in Christ my saviour sweet
>> That we in Heaven together shall meet
>> When Angels shall with Trumpets say
>> Arise Ye Dead and come away.

Thomas Timmins, brought down from Staffordshire at the very start of the reclamation of the Exmoor Estate, is undoubtedly the lynch-pin and key to unravelling the mystery of some of John Knight's more ambitious—but uncompleted plans for his property. What wouldn't I give for a glimpse of the maps and plans drawn up by this Land Surveyor, but to date they have not been located, and in all probability have not survived.

Thomas Timmins's home at Simonsbath was White Rock Cottage—adjacent to where the school was later built—and since it is likely that all the early work on John Knight's Exmoor Estate was carried out under his direction, it is likely too that his cottage was one of the first built in Simonsbath since Boevey completed his house in 1654.

We know that Thomas Timmins was still living at White Rock Cottage in 1830, because his name and address is given in a list of subscribers to *The History of Carhampton* by J. Savage, published in that year. We know too from the Winsford Parish Registers that by 1834—despite the fact that many of the projects begun by John Knight were uncompleted—Thomas had returned to Staffordshire and was living at Kings Winford when he came down to Winsford in that year to marry his second wife, Mary Baker.

Thomas Timmins's first wife was not the only person to come down from Sedgely to Exmoor, but whether Edward Smith who arrived at about the same time was related, or even a friend, is not known.

In 1823, Edward Smith married Elizabeth Dallyn of Challacombe at North Molton Church. Their first child was baptised at Challacombe in 1825, where they were then living although Edward was already working at Simonsbath. By the time their second child was born in 1827 they were living in Simonsbath, where Edward was employed as a gardener by John Knight. Two other children were born in Simonsbath in 1830 and 1832; the first of these, Jeremiah, was later the licencee of the lonely Acland Arms at Moles Chamber for many years, combining his duties as a publican with farming. He also looked after the stock on the adjoining Acland Allotment.

Like Thomas Timmins, Edward Smith had moved from Simonsbath by 1834, and was again living in Challacombe when another child was born. He was still employed as a gardener by John Knight but had moved on by 1835.

We have no means now of knowing where Edward Smith and his family lived in Simonsbath, but possibly it was in the row of cottages known as Pound Cottages, the only ones—apart from White Rock Cottage—listed in the Census of 1841. At this date all of the cottages in the village were listed under "Simonsbath", as they were on several occasions in later Census Returns, which makes it extremely difficult to identify individual dwellings.

There is some reason to believe there may have been more cottages in Simonsbath in the early days of John Knight's reclamation than are recorded in the Census of 1841, and in order to obtain a more acceptable view of the "Status Quo" it is necessary to take the statistical Census Returns of 1821 and 1831 into consideration.

In 1821 there were just nine houses recorded on the whole of the former Royal Forest of Exmoor including Simonsbath; with a total population of 125, or whom 113 were males, and 12 females. Ten years later the Census records a total of ten inhabited houses but with population figures of only 52, 31 males and 21 females. This Census also records 20 uninhabited houses. It is not hard to deduce the reason why.

The early stages of John Knight's reclamation, which entailed the use of a considerable labour force, reached its peak in the mid to late 1820s with the import of 200 Irish labourers to work on the construction of Pinkworthy Pond and the canal and railway system, linking Simonsbath with Porlock Weir, but with the abandonment before completion of this and other projects, the demand for labour, and thus accommodation, fell dramatically, and the near balance of male-female population in 1831 suggests that most of the workforce employed by John Knight at this time were married men and their families; a point we will return to shortly.

It is surely not an unreasonable assumption that some of the uninhabited cottages were in Simonsbath itself. Indeed there is evidence that a few of these early cottages—which like Pound Cottages and White Rock were of single storey construction—were converted to use as farm buildings, or vice versa at some time in their history; old fireplaces having been discovered in these buildings. It is also a reasonable conjecture that as two of the three farms created by John Knight—Cornham and Honeymead—had three cottages apiece, then the farm created at the same date at Simonsbath (Barton) would have been similarly equipped, but there is no record of any cottage there in the Census Returns.

The Census of 1841, however, does give some further food for thought because it records that 100 agricultural labourers had left the Forest on Saturday night as was their usual custom, to sleep in adjoining parishes and return on Monday morning, but how many of these men actually lived in Simonsbath during the week is not recorded.

A self-conducted survey of the Church registers of the parishes bordering on to Exmoor Proper for the years 1821-1841 reveals that at least 49 children were born to 26 married couples living on the Moor. Most of the male parents can be identified from John Knight's labour accounts of 1835 and 1836, and the Census of 1841 as being in his employ, and of these the homes of 16 are known. Five of these families were living within the village of Simonsbath, the others in cottages dotted around the Moor. This leaves 10 families unaccounted for, but it is thought that some, like John Knight's gardeners, Edward Smith and John Mark, lived in the village, and possibly his head groom Charles Crowe, though I have a gut feeling that he lived in one of the Honeymead cottages.

In 1819, the licence of the old Simonsbath Inn was transferred from John Hooper—long-time landlord of the inn—to James Davey, and it was during his short stay that six notorious ruffians of the Johnson Gang were apprehended in the village—probably at the inn—and taken to Wilton Gaol to await trial at the next Somerset Assizes, charged with a serious felony at Exford. According to a report in the *Taunton Courier* (27 Jan 1820) Exmoor Forest had long been disturbed by the "bandittii".

The *Taunton Courier's* coverage of the Assizes held at Taunton in April 1820 was farcical. The report stated that only six of the 84 prisoners on trial fitted the description of the Johnson Gang; one of whom was acquitted, no mention is made of the sentence of another; the others were sentenced to death, but reprieved before the judge left town.

A check for the said villains in the Crown Minutes Book held in the Public Record Office revealed that none of the crimes committed by the men named in the *Taunton Courier* took place anywhere in the Exford-Exmoor area; the nearest being at Taunton. Further investigation revealed that the Johnson

*Simonsbath House and John Knight's unfinished Mansion
in late 19th Century.*

Simonsbath House (Lodge) in early 20th Century.

Victorian Ice House adjacent Ashcombe Water.

Pound Cottages (Lower House) and Exmoor Forest Hotel, about 1910.
Mary Elworthy in doorway.

Gang—all from Exford—had caused a "Disturbance of the Peace" on Christmas Day 1819 in Exford and had stolen a purse from James Baker; badly injuring him in the process. All the men were found guilty of the charges against them, but their sentences were not recorded.

We do not know if the Johnson Gang had been frequent visitors to the Simonsbath Inn, but there is a strong suspicion that they were, and this may well have been the reason why James Davey placed an advertisement in the *Exeter Flying Post* (31.8.1820) in a last ditch effort to clean up his reputation and that of the inn. The advertisement reads as follows: *Simonsbath Inn.* "James Davey begs most respectively to acquaint his old friends and the Public that he has fitted out the above inn in a neat and commodious manner for the reception of Gentlemen, travellers etc., where every accommodation may be had at a moderate charge; J. Davey having removed the many obstacles that have hitherto not been to the credit of the house, trusts by these recent alterations to merit their approbation and support". N.B. Good beds and stabling. Simonsbath Aug. 25th 1820.

James Davey does not appear to have been very successful in his plea for approbation and support, and was replaced by Thomas Tipper in the following year. He was to be the last licencee of the Simonsbath Inn while it was based in Boevey's old house, sharing it with Thomas Timmins the farmer. According to the Ale House Returns, Thomas Tipper was still holding the licence in the year 1827/28 but how much longer he remained there is uncertain as there is a gap of several years in the Returns after 1828, but by the time John Knight and his family—who had been living in what afterwards became known as the Castle Hotel, Lynton—took up residence in the old house at Simonsbath in 1830*, Thomas Tipper had moved on; the licence of the inn given up, and for the next 25 years there was no inn within the village of Simonsbath.

Soon after John Knight moved from Lynton to Simonsbath, work was begun on building a large mansion to the rear of the old house and it was probably at around this time that the "Victorian" Ice House was built a short distance away, set into the east bank of Ashcombe Water, adjacent to White Rock Cottage. The Ice House was completed, but not the Mansion House, probably because the money required to finish this project was more urgently needed elsewhere on the Exmoor Estate, where the cost of reclamation and other large schemes had proved far more expensive than John Knight had anticipated; a situation that was not helped when a large inheritance he had been expecting, failed to materialise and passed instead to a female branch of the family.

---

* John Knight was still living at Lynton in Dec. 1829, this being the address given for replies to his advertisements in the *North Devon Journal* and other local papers, re bookings for bullock keep on Exmoor for the following year.

CHAPTER 3

THE DEER PARK AND SHOOTING TOWER

NO LARGE landed estate in John Knight's day was considered complete without its deer park, which was desirable not only for the sport and venison it provided, but also on account of its aesthetic appeal. The Exmoor Estate was no exception, and a large area of rough moorlands adjoining the road leading from Simonsbath towards South Molton in one direction, and Prayway Head on the Brendon road in the other, was set aside for this purpose. It was then well stocked with Fallow Deer, which, along with John Knight's sheep, were considered fair game by some of his labourers and shepherds, who by all accounts, were a pretty wild bunch at that time, and much given to thieving.

Although Prayway Head does not at first sight appear to be the obvious choice of direction in which to expand the deer park, on account of the detour needed around the old farm at Simonsbath, there is ample evidence that this was indeed the case.

Tucked away behind a high beech topped hedge, immediately to the west of the Brendon road, at a point about midway between Simonsbath and Prayway Head stands the remains of a round stone built tower now in rather a collapsed state. The tower is entered from the east through a nicely arched doorway. The inside of the building has a diameter of about 12 ft and in its ruined state a maximum height of 11-12 ft. Some people think the tower was used as an observation post to study the habits of the Fallow Deer, but most of the descendants of long established families on Exmoor believe it once formed part of a deer trap, the deer being shot from the tower, hence its local name of the Shooting or Hunting Tower, but also known as the Round House, or Simonsbath Tower.

There has been considerable speculation over the years as to the purpose for which this little tower was built; some of it—particularly recently—bearing no relation to the evidence on the ground, or in records, and certainly not in the inherited beliefs and traditions of long established Exmoor families. It has therefore been necessary to return to the site and re-examine the area around. This, coupled with research into the way deer parks were run, and a detailed examination of the earliest large scale maps of the area, and last, but by no means least, due consideration to local knowledge and tradition, has convinced me that although I was basically on the right lines in *The Heritage of Exmoor*, I certainly did not do justice to the information at my disposal, and in consequence failed to present a convincing argument. It is my intention here—having been denied that privilege elsewhere—to redress the situation on the basis of what can and what cannot be substantiated.

Of three articles concerning the Simonsbath Tower, or Round House, that appeared in the Exmoor Review in 1989, 1990 and 1991, only one—that by Dr Ernest Mold of Lynton, in 1990—takes into account all of the known factors and makes sense of them, linking the deer park, local tradition as to the purpose of the tower, and a massive wall a short distance to the east— together. He reasoned that the wall was used to guide deer into range of a rifleman standing in the tower, looking out through the doorway; a conclusion with which Hazel Eardley-Wilmot—who accompanied him—was in total agreement in her book *Yesterday's Exmoor*, published in the same year.

The massive wall mentioned by Ernest Mold and Hazel Eardley-Wilmot, was situated along the far side of the field, east of the tower and the Brendon road. Within living memory it stood 9 ft or so in height; heavily buttressed, and the only one of its type on Exmoor. Sadly, much of this old wall, which originally continued southwards to join the northern boundary hedge of the old Simonsbath farm has disappeared, although it can still be traced on the ground. The remaining section of the wall has been reduced to a height of about five feet by the Exmoor Estate workforce, who over the years have found it a convenient quarry.

Research into the way deer parks were run has proved beyond a shadow of doubt that the original height of this wall is consistent with the killing area in other deer parks—nothing else. In early days this was carried out from a hide or ambush. In John Knight's case, from his tower.

The nearest point from tower to wall is less than 200 yards away, and at the corner where the wall turned back to the Brendon road (this section no longer exists but can be plainly seen on early large scale maps) is no more than 250-300 yards away, well within accurate range of a rifle of that period. Moreover, the huge wall was placed in such a way that any animal passing along in front of it would have been in full view from the tower at all times—there were no hedges to obstruct the view then. Had the wall been built any further to the east, closer to Ashcombe Bottom, this would not have been the case; the deer would have dropped out of sight and thus defeated the whole object of the set-up.

Having, I sincerely believe, positively established the connection between the tower and massive wall as the killing area of John Knight's Deer Park, it is, I believe, also possible to date its construction with some accuracy.

In the first instance the only enclosure shown on the Inclosure Map of the Forest of Exmoor 1819, is that around Simonsbath Farm. Therefore the wall does not pre-date the map. Secondly, among John Knight's labour and small bills accounts for 1835 and 36, held in the Kidderminster Reference Library, is James Quartley's bill for repairs to three small sections of a dry stone wall on Great Ashcombe, at a total cost of 9s. 7d. The Inclosure Map defines Great Ashcombe as the area of land north of the old farm at Simonsbath, between the valleys of Limecombe and Ashcombe.

There is only one dry stone wall on Great Ashcombe, namely the massive wall of the Deer Park; the remainder being what is termed in James Quartley's accounts as cased walls—stone faced and filled with earth within.

Therefore the dry stone wall was built at some time between 1820 and 1836, earlier rather than later as the account was for repairs, and if, as believed, wall and tower are contemporary, then both date from before 1836 and were probably built around the time—or shortly before—John Knight took up residence at Simonsbath House in 1830.

In his article published in the 1989 Exmoor Review, Tony Peck put forward a theory that the Round House was linked in with John Knight's scheme to construct a railway from Porlock Weir to Exmoor Forest, using the water from Pinkworthy Pond to power the incline section needed at the Simonsbath end, with a station at the top, as per Dr Youell's article in the 1974 Exmoor Review; although Dr Youell makes no mention of the Round House, nor is it shown on the map of the proposed railway.

Tony Peck goes on to say: "Without going too deeply into the problem of levels, we know the height at which the leat had to start its journey from Pinkworthy Pond, and having made allowances for keeping the water flowing on its 3 mile course, we know the level at which it was intended to round the head of Lime Combe. Continuing on at that level the leat would be travelling south-east and heading straight for the Round House. In short the Round House was intended to mark the eastern terminal of the leat from Pinkworthy Pond and was built for that purpose in C1826."

What Tony Peck has tried to do is to make certain totally irrelevant facts fit his theory, not the other way round as should be the case. It is not surprising he did not wish to go too deeply into the problem of levels. Had he done so, by taking the trouble to walk a quarter of a mile or so in a north westerly direction away from the tower, across the field in which it stands, and the field above to the hedge that crosses the head of Limecombe—near the sheep pens—he would have found on the north side of this hedge the canal or leat from Pinkworthy Pond, and thus its true level, which indicidentally is a good 20 metres in height above the level he would have it to be. Furthermore it is proven fact that the eastern terminal of the Pinkworthy canal—leat—was nowhere near the tower. The canal continued on along the north side of the hedge above the sheep pens, across the Brendon road, and on above the northern boundary hedge of the Great Ashcombe fields, through the hedge and across Little Ashcombe and Honeymead Allotments, through the fir plantation—where it can still be plainly seen—to end a few yards further on at the very edge of Exe Cleave; south of Warren Farm and the river.*

Tony Peck goes on to suggest that because of their standing and lack of alternative accommodation at the time, the surveyors working on this project would have lodged at John Knight's house in Simonsbath, and that the Round House was built as a surveyor's house, their base camp, the Portakabin of the day.

Unfortunately this does not stand up either. In the first instance Thomas Timmins—John Knight's surveyor—had his own accommodation at White

---

* See *The Heritage of Exmoor* for further details.

The Shooting Tower, Author and Friend.

Remains of once-massive boundary wall of the killing area of John Knights deer park.

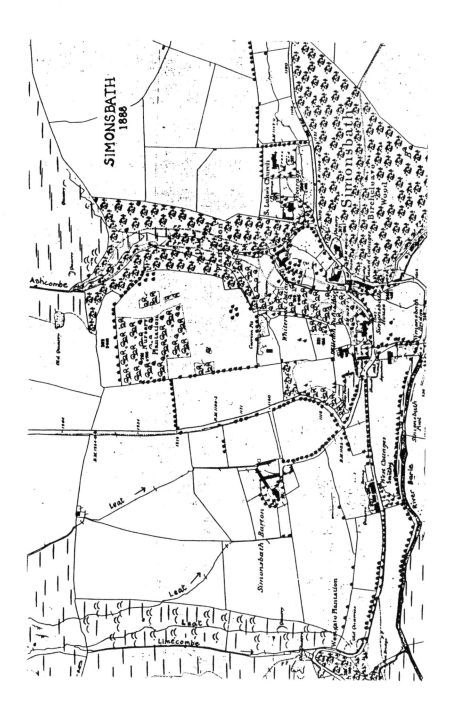

SIMONSBATH
1888

Rock Cottage. Secondly there would have been no point whatsoever in building a "surveyors' house" where the tower is sited, or to bring the leat there. This was not the site of the Limecombe Station, where the proposed railway from Porlock Weir was to link with a water powered inclined plane down to the Simonsbath Station, which would have been close to where West Gate Cottages now stand.

In the 1991 Exmoor Review, Tim Davey O.B.E., added his thoughts to the subject. He did not believe that the Knights, father and son, hard headed businessmen, were the kind of people to spend a not inconsiderable sum on erecting a store for surveying equipment likely to be in use for only a year or two, nor could it have been of any use as a site office—sentiments with which I entirely agree. He continues with: "As for its use as some kind of hide when culling deer, surely the same argument applies 'a fortiori' when the necessary hole or other structure could be far more cheaply constructed?"

Tim Davey assumes that because his first argument is valid then his second must be also, but this is not so. There is a world of difference between the way in which the Knight family conducted their business affairs and the way in which they indulged their pleasures, where no expense was ever spared, as any student of the Knight family history will tell you; and, having spent a considerable sum on enclosing a deer park and stocking it with deer, I cannot see John Knight, his sons, or his guests sitting it out in a hole in the ground or in a cheap and nasty squat, waiting for the deer to come within range, when, for the sake of a few £'s more, a small and better suited, warm and dry building could be erected for the same purpose.

In his article, Tim Davey suggests the most likely use for the little tower was as an explosives store, this being a regular requirement when digging foundations for new buildings, new roads, and removing large rocky outcrops and so on, the building being admirably designed for this purpose.

Contrary to Tim Davey's opinion, there is not a shred of evidence to support this view, and though no records as to the quantities of rock blasting powder used in the early days of reclamation have been discovered, we do know from John Knight's labour and small bills accounts of 1835 and 36, that all the blasting powder required at that time was purchased as and when needed from Thomas Greenslade, shopkeeper of Red Lion, Exford. There is no reason to believe there was any different arrangement earlier. Moreover, it was not compulsory before the 1870s to have a powder magazine or explosives store, and it was by no means unusual to find gun powder etc., stored in the room of a house, preferably where there was some heat to keep the powder dry. Nothing has been found to indicate that Thomas Greenslade had an explosives store, separate and away from his house, even though Red Lion was on the edge of the village of Exford.

For the same reason it is hardly likely that John Knight would have gone to the trouble and unnecessary expense of building a special store for explosives on the site where the tower stands. It would not have been of much use there.

Tim Davey concludes his article by referring to Dr Mold's account of the old Lynton man, (not Simonsbath man as he writes) who in his youth walked the old moorland track from Lynton to Simonsbath and became completely lost in the desolate upland when the mist thickened, and of his great relief when he saw the old shooting tower just ahead. For no other reason, apparently, than to try and give some credence to his theory, Tim Davey substitutes shot tower for shooting tower, though what he hoped to achieve I cannot imagine. There is a world of difference between a shooting tower and a shot tower, and neither has anything to do with an explosives store.

That the tower could have been used for other purposes over the years is not disputed. The most likely use would appear to have been as a game larder, for which it would have been ideal and appropriate, because when John Knight took over the major part of the old Royal Forest and adjoining manor of Brendon—and for many years after—Exmoor and the surrounding moorland commons were abounding with Black Game (Grouse).

In *Notes by the Way* in the *West Somerset Free Press* dated 15.2.1974, Jack Hurley has this to say about the tower. "I must tell readers interested in the origin of the old tower at Barton Farm, Simonsbath, that the 'hunting tower' theory seems to have been demolished by a note that has reached me from Mr L. G. Graham, a retired farmer living near Porlock. Mr Graham says that his father was working for Sir Frederic Knight between 1880 and 1890 when the tower was built and that it was intended as a kiln for drying grass. The project, Mr Graham adds, "was a failure".

While I do not for a moment doubt Mr Graham's integrity, I do believe he was misinformed by his father as to the date the tower was built. If, on the evidence presented, it is accepted that the dry stone wall on Great Ashcombe repaired by James Quartley in 1836 is the massive wall referred to earlier and that this wall is contemporary with the tower, then it predates that year, but the earliest documented evidence concerning the tower discovered to date appears in an advertisement in the *North Devon Journal* 1.5.1862, when the Round House Field, 30 acres in extent, was one of several lots in a grass sale at Simonsbath Barton.

Replies to letters sent to Tim Davey and Tony Peck—voicing concern over their articles in the Exmoor Review—were less than helpful to their cause. In the first instance Tim Davey could not understand why I (and I might add, many others) should be upset by folk speculating in print about the antecedents of that interesting little tower. He ends his letter with 'Does it really matter in 1991 what it was built for?'.

If it does not matter to Mr Davey what the tower was built for, why did he bother to write his article in the first place? Moreover, it is hardly the trivial matter he would have it to be but very much a part of our Exmoor heritage. No useful purpose is served by unwarranted speculation of this nature. It does not promote the cause of Exmoor's history: only confuses the issues concerned.

In a remarkably frank and detailed letter, Tony Peck has sought to justify his stand on the Simonsbath Tower. He tells me that having spent some time working on the Exmoor Estate some 20-30 years before, he had became acquainted with all the local folk lore. Fair comment, but of the six informants he names, only two were from long established Exmoor families and the views he expresses are not the opinions of these two men.

Tony goes on to explain the prime reason for his article; of his love of stonework and his concern for the wellbeing of the tower, which was—and still is—in danger of total collapse, and of his hopes that with the right kind of publicity, someone, somewhere, would do something about preserving it, and as he could not support the shooting tower theory as he had never been able to understand how it would work, he took his own line, as per his article in the 1989 *Exmoor Review*.

Much as I admire Tony Peck's motives in regard to the preservation of the Simonsbath Tower, no evidence has been forthcoming to support his theory. Sadly too, despite his efforts, he did not achieve his objective. It is to be hoped that in the light of what is now known about the tower that something will be done to preserve this historic little building.

In the interest of what is sincerely believed to be the authentic history of Simonsbath Tower, and ever hopeful that the co-editors of the Exmoor Review would eventually allow me a little space to clarify the issue in a proper democratic manner (earlier attempts having failed) a further letter was sent to the appropriate place on the 25th July 1991. This letter included details of my correspondence to Tim Davey and Tony Peck, along with their replies; also my research findings on the way deer parks were constructed and run, as extracted from Whitehead's *Deer and Their Management in the Deer Parks of Great Britain*, which provides irrefutable evidence that when John Knight built his shooting tower and the massive wall close by, he was merely setting out the killing area of his deeer park in the time honoured traditional manner.

As there has been no reply to my letter, and nothing further has appeared in later publications by the Exmoor Society, it is to be presumed that despite the evidence to the contrary, the co-editors of the Exmoor Review still wish the tower issue to remain—as they have declared it—"a matter of speculation". That is their privilege. I leave it to my readers to come to their own conclusions.

Footnote. By the late 1840s the herd of Fallow Deer in John Knight's deer park had increased in numbers to the stage where they could no longer be contained within the park, and had in consequence become a pest, doing considerable damage to crops on Frederic Knight's newly created tenanted farms and much further afield. This was damage that had to be paid, or allowed for, and with repeated demands for compensation becoming an ever increasing burden on diminishing resources, the decision was made to rid the Moor of these pests and within a few years they were totally eradicated.

CHAPTER 4

SPORTING ACTIVITIES—CONTEMPORARY BUILDINGS

SPORTING activities indulged in by the Knight family were by no means confined to their deer park. John Knight's three sons, Frederic, Charles and Lewis, who grew up in Lynton and Simonsbath, were all notable sportsmen in their day. All were crack shots who could put a bullet into a penny piece at 12 paces, and with an abundance of game and vermin on the Exmoor and Brendon Estates at their disposal, were never short of a target on which to practise their skills.

The Knight brothers were all exceptional horsemen, who for wild and reckless daring in their youth had no equal, and mounted as they were on the finest horses money could buy, were extremely hard to keep up with when out hunting, whether the quarry was the red deer or the fox.

Fishing on the rivers of Exmoor was strictly preserved by the Knights, so presumably they were also accomplished fishermen.

John Knight was a subscriber to the old pack of Exmoor Staghounds, a pack that his son Frederic had hunted with as a boy, but due to a change in hunting style by the then Master—which displeased many of the local landowners and subscribers—the pack was sold off in 1825, and though a new pack was formed two years later, hunting over the next 30 years was sporadic, with frequent changes of Masters. In some years there was no hunting at all. At such times poachers took a heavy toll on the deer population and had it not been for one or two far-sighted landowners, particularly John and Frederic Knight, who set aside a part of the Brendon Estate at Scob Hill, and there strictly preserved the deer, there would have been very few deer to hunt when hunting was resumed on a more regular basis in the mid-1850s.

Local tradition has it that the opening meet of the staghounds was held at Simonsbath, with the hounds being brought there the day before and housed overnight for the occasion, and though no record has been found to confirm that this was so in John Knight's day, there was certainly a fine set of kennels at Simonsbath at that time, much of which has survived, including the building containing the copper furnace for boiling up carcasses for the hounds, though this, and all the other buildings there have long been put to other use.

The whole set-up appears far too elaborate to have been built just for the occasional overnight kennelling of the staghounds, and seeing as how the pack was restarted in 1827, only two years after the old pack was disposed of, and being as it was around the time that John Knight was preparing to take up residence at Simonsbath, one wonders if it was his intention to establish a permanent pack of hounds there. Assuredly the kennels, which covered a ground area of more than 4,300 square feet, about half of which was roofed over and divided into at least seven compartments, some with raised floors, was more than adequate for the few gun dogs, terriers etc., required for normal sporting activities on the estate.

The kennels are not shown on the plan of Simonsbath House and Farm drawn up when the Forest was surveyed in 1815, and appear to date—like so many of John Knight's major projects—from around the late 1820s. Repairs to the kennels were carried out in November 1836 by James Jewell a mason; and a labourer, who spent two days there at a total labour cost of 9/-.

The first meet of the Devon and Somerset Staghounds at Simonsbath of which record has been found is that of the 30th October 1848, when a fine hind was raised in the Old Deer Park and after a first class run—with the pace such that few could stay with the hounds—the hind was eventually killed near Cow Castle*.

Nothing further has been discovered concerning meetings of the Staghounds at Simonsbath until the 7th September 1854, when the *North Devon Journal* records that the hounds met there for the third time in as many weeks, and a stag was taken on each occasion. The last, a fine five-year-old, was caught alive and reserved uninjured for the Barnstaple hunt meeting.

The three meetings in as many weeks indicate that Simonsbath was the venue for the opening meet of the Staghounds at that time, and remained so for several years.

The opening meet at Simonsbath in 1855 was attended by about 70 riders 'of the right sort'. A hind was raised but after a capital run escaped. A splendid old stag was not so lucky. He was taken in the water near Malmsmead after a fine run lasting 58 minutes.*

Newspaper reports on staghunting on Exmoor prior to 1860 when the *West Somerset Free Press* came into production are few and far between, nor was the situation much improved for a few years thereafter, but there was one letter in the edition of the latter paper, dated 31st August 1862, by a 'lover of the sport' which describes the opening meet of the Staghounds at Simonsbath in that year, when nearly 100 well mounted riders took to the field.

On this occasion no deer was to be found on the North Forest, so Mr Snow (of Oare Manor) the 'old invincible' and much respected sportsman, tried over Oare Common where a herd of seven or eight was found, but being disturbed by passers-by they left before the hounds were in place. At length a fine hind sprung up and away towards Larkbarrow. After giving her 40 minutes grace the hounds were laid on, it then being half-past-one.

Away went the hind over hill and dale to the North Forest where it was very bad travelling, and on to the Simonsbath-Brendon road—where a good view was got by hounds and men—and on to Farley, where for a short time she was surrounded by hounds in the water there, before breaking away across the summit of Cheriton Ridge and back to Badgworthy, by which

* *The Chase of the Wild Red Deer.* C. S. Collyns. 1862.
* *North Devon Journal* 23.8.1855.

time only six or so of the hundred riders who started out, were still with her, the heavy going over the moors having emptied many a saddle. Leaving Oare to the left the hind took away to Chalk Water and thence to Weir Water, and then by Frederic Knight's tram road to the Lynton-Porlock road. At this point the hounds came to check, it being excessively hot and fast work. By this time both the hounds and the remaining horsemen had had quite enough. There were only four or five riders still with the hounds when they were called off after a hard gallop lasting for three hours.

It is not now the custom to hunt hinds in August; the season for hind hunting begins in November and ends in March, but in the old days, particularly when deer were scarce, it was not unusual for a hind or two to be hunted at the beginning of the staghunting season, to get the hounds in trim.

The report given above is the last reference found in local newspapers as to Simonsbath being the venue of the opening meet of the Devon and Somerset Staghounds. The first meet recorded in the following year was for the 4th September, which was held at Hawkridge. The same applies to 1863 and 1864, but in 1865 the opening meet was held at Cloutsham. It has been held there ever since.

Although there is little doubt that the foxhounds were also frequently at Simonsbath, records of meets there are also few and far between. One such meeting, held on the 18th November 1862 proved to be an exceptional day, which resulted in a letter to the *North Devon Journal* (27.11.62) entitled—A run with the North Devon Hounds, the gist of which is as follows:

"The meet at Simonsbath was held on a lovely hunting morning after a slight frost, with a good field in attendance. Cornham Brake was drawn; it was a good drag and the fox which was evidentally in his earth—left there. Titchcombe Valley was drawn next, where the hounds got on to the line of a fox and it was a treat to see the way they held on to it across Exe Head and on to the top of Oar Oak Vale, where he was marked in a shallow earth. What a thrill diffused through the field. For miles around the eyes rested on an expanse of heath and heather and a clipping run was certain. There never was a more thoroughly sporting scene than that portrayed at that moment, etc., etc.

The hounds were then taken to the adjoining combe where a fine dog fox bolted down the combe to Cheriton Ridge and on to Fursehill, Shallowford, Woolhanger Cottage, Blackburrow and Swincombe Rocks, and was finally run into in Challacombe Village without having had a check for an instant. A fine run indeed."

In following a few of the meetings of the Devon and Somerset Staghounds held at Simonsbath along with that of the North Devon Hounds we have gone far ahead of developments in the village, some of which were contemporary with the sporting scene.

Stables were built to house John Knight's fine stock of thoroughbred horses. According to one or two of Simonsbath's older inhabitants, the old stables belonging to Simonsbath House were those adjacent to White Rock

Cottage, in the building now being used as a store and toilets for visitors to the adjoining car park, but if these were—as believed—the Higher Stables referred to in John Knight's labour accounts for February 1836, when John Ash, a mason, was paid £2.17.1½ for paving the floor, and a further £2.15.7½ for other work at these stables, then it is clear there were already other stables in use, probably nearer the house. John Ash's account represents some 50 days' work at the Higher Stables at the 2s.3d. a day he was paid as a mason. This was no minor repair job, but the major construction of a new building.

In addition to the "Higher Stables", James Jewell was busy constructing a "Colt's Shead"—completed by the end of 1836; presumably built to house the progeny of John Knight's thoroughbred horses. This building was roofed over with heath (heather) by Ambrose Ridd, a thatcher from Challacombe, who laid on 17 square of thatch at a cost of 1s.9d. a square.* We have no means of knowing where this building stood, or if it has survived in a different form.

There is every reason to believe that a smithy was also built in the village at an early date. The labour accounts of 1835 and 36 record the shoeing of oxen as well as horses, although there may not have been a resident blacksmith in the village at this time. Several blacksmiths' names are recorded, most of whom can be traced to villages around the Moor. It would appear that they came to Simonsbath as and when their services were required, and returned home when their work was completed.

In an interesting article concerning John Knight's Exmoor Estate, which appeared in the *Taunton Courier* on 23rd September, 1840, yet another sport, that of hawking, is highlighted. The relevant paragraph is as follows: "On passing over the Moor last Saturday we were much struck on seeing a gentleman coming down the hill towards Simonsbath, with a hawk hooded in his hand and equipped as a falconer, with an attendant carrying a dead bird which had been killed by the hawk. The falconer proved to be one of Mr Knight's sons, who had devoted considerable attention to the ancient pastime, which he had been endeavouring to revive, but with what success we are unable to say as the young gentleman does not seem desirous to communicate the results of his experiments."

The correspondent responsible for the article then paid tribute to John Knight for his efforts in preserving the old red deer: He goes on to say, "We saw a brace of sturdy Irishmen clad in 'frieze' clothing and armed with formidable looking shelleleghs, who told us that they and several of their countrymen are engaged as gamekeepers on the Forest at 12/- a week and a 'shoot' of clothes each".

According to Rev. W. H. Thornton, first vicar of the parish of Exmoor, writing in 1897, Frederic Knight was accustomed to taking peregrines from their nests in the Exmoor Country and training them himself. He was a member of the Hawking Club, whose headquarters were at The Hague.

* A square = 10ft x 10ft.

CHAPTER 5

SIMONSBATH BECOMES A TRUE VILLAGE

HAVING described the birth of the village of Simonsbath and written about some of its early inhabitants, it is now time to move on to the next stage in its development, which is its growth from a small hamlet into a proper village, with church, school, inn, post office and shop and resident tradesmen, although this did not take place in John Knight's lifetime and some years were yet to pass before such a village became a reality.

Despite the major changes wrought to the face of Exmoor by John Knight, he in fact spent very little time living there. In the first ten years following his purchase of the Exmoor Estate he chose to live at Lynton and it was not until 1830 that he took up residence at Simonsbath, and soon after, when his wife's health began to fail, their winters were spent in Rome.

In 1837, on the advice of the family physician, Dr Sully, John Knight and his wife left Simonsbath to live in Jersey where it was thought Mrs Knight would benefit from the milder climate. It was not to be, for according to a report in the *Taunton Courier* (6.8.1838) Dr Sully of Oakhill near Taunton, left town on Tuesday morning last, express to her assistance, a violent cold having affected a return of her distressing condition (not specified).

It was probably also on Dr Sully's advice that the couple left Jersey in the following year to take up permanent residence in Rome, but sadly Mrs Knight's health continued to deteriorate and she died there two years later. John Knight, now an old man of 75, turned over the management of the Exmoor and Brendon Estates to his eldest son Frederic in the same year, and remained in Rome until his own death in 1850, leaving the two estates, which were now burdened with substantial mortgages, to Frederic, along with other property in Worcestershire, but very little money, as he had left too large a fortune to his other two sons and three daughters. Unfortunately for Frederic Knight his father no longer had that kind of money, which placed a further burden on his shoulders and one that was to give him many a sleepless night before the matter was finally resolved some 14 years later, and the last of the money due to his brothers and sisters paid up.

A look at the Census of 1841 reveals that none of the Knight family were in residence at Simonsbath; the old house having been left in the charge of Sarah Howchin, wife of William, butler and general factotum to the Knights. He too was absent from home, but there were five other servants living in the house at this time, three females and two males. In all probability Frederic Knight was away on business concerning his election as a Member of Parliament for West Worcestershire; a seat he was to hold for the next 44 years.

In the year of his father's death, Frederic Knight married. Shortly after, he sold his father's prime breeding stock of 40 thoroughbred horses, along with 20 carthorses and a similar number of Exmoor ponies; the sale realizing nearly £1,000. In the following year, the contents of Simonsbath House were sold, along with surplus agricultural machinery. The house was then let to Charles Le Blanc of Epsom with 600 acres for a farm; and let once more with less land before Frederic Knight re-occupied it some 10 years after it was first let. In the meantime, whenever he and his wife came down to Exmoor, they, like his parents before him, took up residence in Lynton.

By the time the Census of 1851 was recorded a number of farms had been created on the Exmoor Estate and let, and in many cases let again when early tenants found they had bitten off more than they could chew, and after exhausting their limited resources were forced to move on.

In Simonsbath itself there was now a total of seven cottages, one of which—possibly White Rock—was uninhabited at this time. Two more cottages were in the course of construction.

Of the occupants of the cottages listed in the Census of 1841, only one, John Ash—a groom—remained. Nevertheless, the Census is not without interest because it was around this time that the first of a number of families who were to be long associated with the village, began to settle there, and with the help of later Census Returns, Kellys Directories for Somerset, Frederic Knight's Rent Rolls, Parish Registers, Electoral Rolls and other sources, it has been possible to put together what is believed to be a fairly accurate account of who was who and for the most part where they lived. Our main interest is centered on the longer term inhabitants of the village, but there are a few others, who although they may have lived there for only a few short years, did, nonetheless, have a part to play in the making of the history of the village, and these too will be included as we come to them.

Some of the people we will be encountering were already established in Exmoor long before the Census of 1851, though not then living in Simonsbath. William Court was such a man.

In 1841, William Court, then a single labourer, was living in one of the Honeymead Cottages, where he met and fell in love with Charlotte Wyatt who was living in one of the adjoining cottages. They were married at Exford in 1843, and by 1851 were living at Simonsbath Farm (Barton) which had come in hand the year before. William Court was now the father of three children and was one of Frederic Knight's more trusted employees; herdsman and forester, responsible for attending the local markets in the early spring of each year to take bookings for cattle, sheep and horses to summer pasture on the unlet parts of the Exmoor Estate, and then to look after them.

William Court's stay at Simonsbath Farm was a short one, because in the following year it was re-let and the family then moved into a newly completed cottage at the west end of a row of three, above and at right angles to the range of cottages known as Pound Cottages.

Having established where William Court was living in Simonsbath it is necessary to leave him for a moment in order to place the other characters— so to speak—living in the village at this time.

At the eastern end of the same row of cottages lived William Kingdom the blacksmith, with his wife Catherine and son William age 12. William Kingdom senior, who was one of the blacksmiths listed in John Knight's Labour Accounts of 1836, was away from home when the Census of 1851 was taken, but there was a second blacksmith—Thomas Parkin—living in.

On the other side of the road leading into Simonsbath House, and north of the above cottages, on the site where the Exmoor Forest Hotel now stands, were—it is believed—two more cottages. In one of these cottages lived William Fry for many years. He was listed in the Census of 1851 as a gardener, and was for some years employed full time as a nurseryman, responsible for raising the countless numbers of beech saplings needed for planting on the bare tops of the many miles of wall and bank hedges that had been erected on the estate, to provide stockproof fences and shelter for livestock in an otherwise treeless landscape. When John Knight purchased his estate in 1818 the only trees standing there—apart from the Hoar Oak— were four ash, three beech, twenty-three sycamores and seven lime pollards; thirty-seven trees in all; all of which had been planted many years before around Boeveys old house and farmstead.

The only plantation directly attributed to John Knight is the 26 acre beech wood on Birch Cleave, and it was left to his son to plant the hedges and provide shelter belts around his farms. Frederic Knight also laid down most of the plantations to be seen on Exmoor today, although for the most part these have been felled and replanted by employees of the Fortescue Estate in more recent times.

William Fry's nursery, some four and three-quarter acres in extent, was situated in a field about a quarter of a mile to the north of Simonsbath House.

In the Census Returns 1861-1891, the cottage next on the list to that of William Fry and his successor was always occupied by a carpenter. If the cottages are in the correct order in 1851, then for a short while this cottage was occupied by a labourer, Joseph Harris and his family. Joseph was another of John Knight's early employees, but by 1861 he had left Exmoor.

There were, however, two carpenters living in the village in 1851. One of these, James Harvey, was at that time living in Simonsbath House, along with William Howchin, the butler, and one other servant, prior to the disposal of the contents of the house and the subsequent letting of house and farm. James Harvey too was an employee of long standing and had been living on Exmoor since at least as early as 1834. In December of that year he was described as a carpenter of Simonsbath in the Exford Parish Registers when his son John was baptised there, but by 1861, this family too had left the Moor.

The other carpenter living in Simonsbath in 1851, was Thomas Hodge, a native of North Molton. It is believed he was living in one of the Pound Cottages with his wife and five children, but had returned to North Molton by 1861.

In the last of the occupied cottages in Simonsbath in 1851, in the cottage listed next to Thomas Hodge, were four single labourers. All were gone by 1861.

There is no mention of White Rock Cottage in the Census of 1851. It is possible it was being refurbished or converted into two or more dwellings. At a later date it was by no means unusual to find three separate families living there.

Thus it was in 1851. Out of a total population of 35 living within the village, nine were under the age of ten. Probably at that date most or all of the tradesmen were still on Frederic Knight's payroll, but within a few years some were in business on their own account, though no doubt still relying heavily on his custom.

No mention has yet been made of the sawmill and ancillary buildings in Simonsbath, the reason being that no record of the date of its construction has been discovered. There was certainly a sawmill and chaffhouse on this site in Frederic Knight's time and there is reason to believe the original buildings were erected by his father.

Although we know there was a chaffcutter in these buildings when Lord Fortescue took over the Exmoor and Brendon Estates in 1897, it does not necessarily follow that the huge quantities of chaff cut by William Ash (John Knight's Labour Accounts 1835 and 36) was carried out in the chaffhouse there. The operation could have been done by horsepower elsewhere, or even by hand, although because of the huge quantities involved, the latter would appear most unlikely.

No evidence has been forthcoming that the water power at the mill was ever used for grinding corn. On the contrary, in view of the large amounts of oatmeal purchased by John Knight from William Escott, miller of Exford, at this date, this too seems unlikely. By this time, John Knight's vision of rolling acres of golden wheat had faded in the face of the inhospitable Exmoor climate, and such corn as was now grown was mainly oats, which for the most part were not threshed out, but put through the chaffcutter in the sheaf, thus providing a valuable source of feed for his livestock, particularly his horses.

Water to the mill was provided from two sources. One, via a leat from high up Ashcombe Water, was stored ready for use in a millpond which was situated just above what is now Boevey's Restaurant, formerly a cartshed, but one that was not there in Boevey's day, although the old Wool Chamber just to the east of it—now converted into holiday flats—could well have been.

The leat from Ashcombe also supplied water to the kennels and to Simonsbath House for many years. The same source is still used in the house, although the water is now piped in.

There are signs of another millpnd just above the mill—below the main road. A leat from this spot ran parallel to, and just below the Simonsbath-Challacombe road as far as Bale Water, taking in the water from Limecombe along the way. At Bale Water the leat crossed the road and picked up the stream close to where the old track crossed into the cottage-cum-farm there.* Further up this valley, following the eastern tributary running up

* Now the kennels of the Exmoor Foxhounds.

through Tangs Bottom there are signs of another of John Knight's uncompleted projects. It was here, it is believed, he intended to dam the stream in much the same way as he did at Pinkworthy Pond. He would then have been able to release additional water as and when needed into the stream and thus into the leat to the mill, ensuring an adequate supply of water, even in times of severe drought.

The arrival of three large mining concerns on Exmoor in the mid-1850s, following the discovery of a number of promising iron lodes on the Exmoor Estate, provided a much needed boost to the local economy, and though initial hopes of quickly obtaining vast quantities of iron ore were soon dashed, and by the late 1850s-early 1860s all three companies had left Exmoor, it was, nonetheless, during the few short years they were at work there that Simonsbath at last became a village in its true sense.

With the influx of a large number of miners, accommodation was at a premium, with every householder for miles around with a spare room taking in miners as lodgers. Six miner's cottages were also built at Cornham Ford, but by the time they were completed mining on Exmoor was in decline.

Elsewhere in and around the village of Simonsbath, farm and other buildings were converted to temporary barracks for the miners, reverting to their former use after they had left the Moor.

It could well have been around this time that the main building in the group across the road, east of what is now and has for many years been the Exmoor Forest Hotel, was converted for use as miners' accommodation. During recent renovations a fireplace was discovered there, and some of the older inhabitants of Simonsbath can remember a proper flight of stairs leading to a room in the roof space, but this is believed to have been put in at a later date by Charlie Elworthy, farmer and carpenter, who used this room as a workshop.

The first major change to village life in Simonsbath was when an existing cottage was licensed as an inn in 1855; there having been no inn within the village since the late 1820s, when, shortly before John Knight took up residence in Boevey's old house, the inn there was vacated and the licence given up. It is likely it would have remained a 'dry' village had it not been for the arrival of a large number of thirsty miners.

According to William Hannam, in his diary*, the first tenant of the new Simonsbath Inn was constantly in trouble for keeping a disorderly house, and on Lady Day 1856 he was replaced by Hannam's brother-in-law Samuel Gifford. Samuel was of the mind to build a bakehouse at the inn and expressed his desire to Robert Smith—Frederic Knight's Agent—who said that this was also their intention. Robert Smith had also drawn up plans for a "Splendide Hotel" in the village, on the site of premises then used as workshops, and had this plan materialised, Simonsbath Inn would have reverted to a dwellinghouse and shop.

Nothing came of Robert Smith's grandiose plans for his "Splendide Hotel"

* *The Reclamation of Exmoor Forest.* C. S. Orwin and R. J. Sellick. 1970.

and it was some time before the bakehouse was built at the inn. The bakehouse appears to have been a private venture by Henry Scale[1], Superintendant of the Dowlais Mining Company's operations on Exmoor, who after some hard bargaining agreed to let it to Samuel Gifford for £10 a year.

Within a short time Samuel had worked up a good business, whereupon Henry Scale and Robert Smith tried to persuade him to buy the bakehouse, but he declined to do so and was given a week's notice to quiet the premises, and at the end of the week gave up the key. Scale and Smith then tried hard to attract a new tenant, but without success, and at the end of 12 months Samuel Gifford was able to renew his tenancy. He continued in business as innkeeper, shopkeeper and baker until 1860, when, probably as a result of declining business following the departure of the miners, he gave up all the premises he had been renting and left Simonsbath.

The next tenant of the Simonsbath Inn was John Haskings, who is described in the Census of 1861 as an innkeeper, grocer and baker, born at South Molton. He was employing a journeyman baker with the rather grand sounding name of John Le Duc, but by Lady Day 1862 Hoskings had returned to South Molton, where, according to the *North Devon Journal*, he was made bankrupt in September of the same year.

There had been some speculation as to where the Simonsbath Inn of this period was situated, but a careful study of the 1888 25″ O.S. map of Simonsbath and Census Returns of later date has led me to believe that it was at the higher end of the row of Pound Cottages, with the blacksmith's shop parting it from two more cottages at the lower end of the same row— now and for some years past one cottage. We will go into more detail shortly as the history of Simonsbath unfolds.

By the time Robert Holcombe took over the tenancy of the inn and other premises in 1862, the licence had been given up, and it was now known as the "Refreshment House" with only soft drinks to be had there. It is believed that the prime reason for the loss of licence was Frederic Knight's strong aversion to beer and spirits, because of the detrimental effect they had on his men's work and pockets, and thus their ambitions to better themselves.

Robert Holcombe had been working as a mason on Exmoor from at least 1849, when he married Elizabeth Long at Exford. According to the same parish registers he was living in Simonsbath in 1853 when his son William died, and was in all probability living in the middle cottage of the row of three above and at right angles to Pound Cottages and the Simonsbath Inn, with William Court on one side of him and William Kingdom on the other.

By 1861, Robert was combining his work as a mason with farming some 32 acres of land rented from Frederic Knight, which he retained when he took over Simonsbath Inn a year later. There is some reason to believe he also retained the dwelling house he had been living in for at least a part of the time he remained in Simonsbath.

In an advertisement placed in the *North Devon Journal* on the 5.6.1862, Robert Holcombe of the Refreshment House Simonsbath "Begs to inform those gentlemen who intend visiting the sublime scenery and very romantic beauty of the Forest of Exmoor that he has the privilege of granting gentlemen THE FISHING OVER UPWARDS OF ELEVEN MILES of some of the most superb trout streams in the neighbourhood and can supply them with the most superior accommodation at very moderate charges. Good stabling for horses and lock up coach houses.''

The superior accommodation offered in no way tallies with what is known of the Simonsbath Inn cum Refreshment House at that date which is one of the reasons for believing that when Robert Holcombe became the tenant of the inn he retained the cottage he had been living in close by, thus doubling the number of rooms available for letting to visitors.

As far as the fishing is concerned, this is the first record we have of Frederic Knight granting such a privilege to the tenant of the Inn-cum-Refreshment House, but later tenants did have the same right.

The advertisement in the *North Devon Journal* does not appear to have attracted sufficient new business to encourage Robert Holcombe to remain in Simonsbath, and in 1864 he left to take the tenancy of the Sportsmans Inn at Sandyway. His successor at the Refreshment House was James Fry and his wife Elizabeth, who were married at North Molton shortly before they came to Simonsbath to live, but although they took over the Refreshment House, bakehouse and grocer's shop, and the land that Robert Holcombe had been renting, nothing has been found to suggest that they had any spare accommodation to let, despite having no family for many years.

We will return to James Fry later, also William Fry—Frederic Knight's nurseyman—who were not—as once thought—brothers and may not even have been related. In the meantime we need to catch up on other developments taking place in Simonsbath that were to result in it becoming a proper village at last, some 35 years after John Knight built his first cottage there.

With the rise in population on Exmoor brought about by the creation of a number of new farms and cottages to service them, increased still further by the arrival of a considerable number of miners in the mid-1850s, the time was deemed right to implement the last requirement of the Disafforestation of Exmoor Act of 1815, which had made provision for the erection of a church and parsonage when the population was considered large enough to warrant them. By the autumn of 1856 both buildings had been erected on the 12 acres of land reserved by the Crown for this purpose, and with the appointment of the first minister, the ecclesiastical and civil parish of Exmoor was born. Anyone requiring the services of a parson beforehand turned to one of the adjoining parishes; and Exford, being the nearest to Simonsbath, was the usual choice.

The church at Simonsbath, dedicated to St Luke, with a seating capacity of 203 people, was consecrated on the 21st October, 1856, by the Bishop, Lord Aukland, to serve the inhabitants of the largest parish in Somerset.

The first encumbent of St Lukes was the Rev. W. H. Thornton, a close friend and confidant of Frederic Knight and his wife. He had previously held the curacy of Lynton and Lynmouth, along with Countisbury, for which he held sole responsibility.

St. Lukes Church C.1910.

St. Lukes Church today.

The Vicarage C.1910.

The Vicarage today with the Knight family tomb in the foreground.

According to the Rev. Thornton in his reminiscences published in 1897, inferior materials were used in the construction of the church. Heavy rains, followed by severe frosts did considerable damage to the Bath Stone it was built with, causing it to flake off by the cartload. Shortly after, a gale took away slates by the hundred from the roof, as a result of iron nails being used—which quickly rusted—instead of copper nails as specified.

Inside the vicarage there were further problems, with the Rev. Thornton having to replace faulty locks and fittings at his own expense. This, coupled with the work that had to be done to establish his garden— walls to build, rocks to clear, paths to make and shrubs and trees to stock his garden—made vast inroads into his stipend, which at £150 a year was not great when the lifestyle he was expected to maintain was taken into consideration, and had it not been for the generosity of his father it is doubtful if he could have afforded to remain there.

Within twelve months of the consecration of the church a school was built in Simonsbath. The promotors were Frederic Knight and the Rev. Thornton, who were both great believers in the education of the working classes. The school was built by public subscription, and at the time of its completion no debt or charge remained on it. The National Society helped by giving £5 towards the school fittings.

There was already a Dame School in Simonsbath when the Rev. Thornton became the vicar of Exmoor. It is described in the Parish Magazine of 1926 as having been held in what was now the kitchen of George Webber's cottage, and the sitting room of Mrs White's cottage, which in the days the Dames School was held there, were three cottages by a different arrangement. The cottages referred to were in fact those at White Rock, on to which the school was built in 1857.

Most of the teaching at the new school in its early days was apparently carried out by the Rev. Thornton himself, with the help of an assistant teacher, Miss Emma Reed from Chawleigh.

In the year the school was completed, the Rev. Thornton married, and soon found that much as he loved his moorland parish, it was far from being the ideal place in which to raise a family, as it was some 11 miles away from the nearest doctor at South Molton, and, following the death of his first daughter only a few short months after his wife gave birth, it is hardly surprising that she began to fret. A second daughter was born in 1859, but in this instance Mrs Thornton had taken the wise precaution to return home to her parents at Larkbeare for the birth.

For a short time after the birth of her daughter, Mrs Thornton appears to have been reasonably contented living in Simonsbath. This was due in no small part to the fact that the Thorntons now had friends of their own standing living there; Mr Torr—an old college friend of the Rev. Thornton—who soon after his arrival married the vicar's niece. They were living at Simonsbath House, Mr Torr having taken the tenancy of the house on Lady Day 1858, along with 120 acres of land, following the departure of Charles Le Blanc, who had been there since 1851. For the past two years Mr Torr had also been assisting the Rev. Thornton with his duties, in the parish and at the school.

The absence of a doctor convenient to Simonsbath was again keenly felt when a major diphtheria epidemic hit the village in 1859; brought there by a girl from Barnstaple who had been hired as a servant. The Thorntons immediately sent their baby daughter and her nurse to a remote farmhouse where they remained for the duration of the epidemic. The rest of the Thornton household promptly went down with diphtheria, all at the same time, and the only apparent cure—a drastic one—was to soak a 'rammer' with sulphuric acid and thrust it down the throat, as necessary, several times a day; the burning effect being relieved with copious libations of Old Port Wine. They eventually recovered, with only one life lost in the village, that of a small baby who could not take the Port and succumbed in consequence.

The diphtheria epidemic, following shortly after by the departure of Mr and Mrs Torr for pastures new, was more than Mrs Thornton could bear, and once again she became very depressed. In normal circumstances she might have soon recovered, but 1860 was the wettest year on record—not conducive to a quick recovery from depression. Moreover, she was pregnant again.

Crisis point was reached on the 11th October 1860, with Mrs Thornton about to give birth to her third child. The vicar was involved in a mad dash across the Moor in the middle of a dark night to fetch the doctor from South Molton, and though the baby was delivered safely, when his wife recovered she became even more desperate to get away from Exmoor, to be nearer a town and a doctor.

Towards the end of the year, the living of Dunsford—a parish between Exeter and Moretonhampstead—came up for sale and was purchased by the Rev. Thornton's father, with vacant possession in February 1861, but one more crisis had to be faced before they could move there, because shortly after Christmas a great fall of snow blocked the roads leading out of Simonsbath to a depth of 11-12ft, and the inhabitants of the village very nearly reduced to starvation. Eventually one or two parties of men managed to get through to Heasley Mill where they were able to purchase two loaves apiece to take home.

A look at the village of Simonsbath and its inhabitants as revealed by the Census of 1861 and Kelly's Directory for the same year, shows us that all of the factors that contribute to the making of a true village had at last come together. It even had its own Post Office and sub-postmaster, in no less a person than Frederic Knight's good and trustworthy servant, William Court. Deliveries of letters at this time were restricted to Tuesdays, and Saturdays, arriving at 12am from South Molton and leaving again at 1.30pm. The nearest money order offices were at Dunster and South Molton.

There does not appear to have been a regular sub-postmaster before William Court took over these duties. According to Henry Scale, writing in July 1856, the letters were then left on a somewhat dirty table at the shop cum inn, but soon after, 1/- a week was being paid for a regular Post Office.

It was probably at this date that William Court became the sub-postmaster, with a room—or part of a room—in his cottage set aside for the Post Office.

It was this William Court who rode over to Porlock in the summer of 1858, following the disappearance of Anna Maria Burgess, the youngest daughter of William Burgess, amidst the strongest suspicions that he had done away with her, to check if she was staying with his sister as he had claimed; a claim that was soon found to be untrue.

By the time that William Court arrived back in Simonsbath with the news, Burgess had left Exmoor and William Fry, the village constable—Frederic Knight's nurseryman—was sent to Lynmouth to see if Burgess had slipped across to South Wales. He had, and shortly after William accompanied Supt. Jeffs of Wiveliscombe, across the Bristol Channel to fetch him back to face trial for the suspected murder of his daughter, even though as yet no body had been found despite a prolonged and thorough search. Eventually, after some months had passed, a reluctant witness came forward and made a statement. This led to the pumping out of the abandoned Wheal Eliza Mine on the banks of the River Barle, about a mile below Simonsbath, and the discovery of poor little Anna Maria's body. Burgess was subsequently hanged for the crime, confessing at the last that he had killed her to save the 2s.6d. a week it was costing him to keep her in lodgings following the death of his wife in the previous year.

We do not know what happened to William Court and his family after 1861, but they were gone from Simonsbath by 1866; Kelly's Directory of that year gives William Shapland as the sub-postmaster. Frederic Knight's Rent Roll of the same year and the Census of 1871 confirms that he was living in William Court's old house. It is possible that the appointment of William Scott as Bailiff on the Exmoor Estate in 1861, following Robert Smith's dismissal as Agent, may have had some bearing on the matter, and it could well be true that William Court was upset by being passed over for the Bailiff's job in the light of his past experience and proven reliability. What is known is that in the early spring of 1862, William Scott also took over William Court's customary duty of attending the local markets in the spring of each year to take bookings for summer pasturage on the Exmoor Estate.

Much has been written about the creation of a number of large farms on the Exmoor Estate in the late 1840s, but less space has been devoted to what became known as the cottage holdings in the village of Simonsbath, and the men who farmed them, and before proceeding further with our history a few observations on how and when these smallholdings came about might not be inappropriate.

A careful study of the earliest of Frederic Knight's surviving Rent Rolls, that of Lady Day 1864, reveals a common factor in all the smallholdings in the village at this time. All had been created out of land surplus to the requirements of Mr Torr when he took the tenancy of Simonsbath House and 120 acres of land in 1858; the former tenant Charles Le Blanc having farmed some 600 acres. All of the newly created smallholdings included 'land late Le Blancs' and therefore do not pre-date the year 1858, although it is possible that the odd field or two around Simonsbath may have been let earlier in this way.

The early tenants of the new smallholdings were for the most part men who had worked on the Exmoor Estate for many years, whose services were no longer required to the extent they once had been now that so much of the estate had been split up into large farms and let, but Frederic Knight was reluctant to lose men of proven ability, most of whom had large families, and he gave them every encouragement to begin farming on their own account and not once was he given cause to regret his decision.

William Fry—Frederic Knight's former nurseryman—was one of the men to profit from this opportunity, and by 1865 he was farming 100 acres. In the same year, he was joined by his father John Fry, who too had spent many years working on the Exmoor Estate, as a shepherd and stockman. The farm was then increased to 217 acres, for which the two men were paying £110.10.0. a year in rent, but though this was a good size farm there is no mention in the Rent Rolls of the usual sources of reference as to what it was called, but in May 1872, when William Fry advertised keep for bullocks and horses in the *North Devon Journal*, the address given was Ashcombe Farm.

In, or shortly before 1871, John Fry, now aged 80 retired from farming. Four years later William Fry gave up the farm and cottage in which he had been living since 1849 and moved to Picked Stones, a farm of 140 acres on the Exmoor Estate—later increased to 163 acres—taking his father with him. John Fry was still living with his son in 1881. He died two years later at the grand age of 93.

William Fry too had retired by 1881 and had passed over his farming interests to his son Charles, who continued to farm at Picked Stones until 1901, when the farm was given up and the Fry family left the Moor.[2]

Returning to the Census of 1861, we find John Kerslake, a carpenter from North Molton, living in what is believed to be the cottage adjoining that of William Fry (listed next to it on the Census Returns 1861-1891). According to the Rev. Thornton, he was the estate carpenter, but he also farmed a little land which had formerly been in the hands of Le Blanc. John Kerslake was still living in the same cottage in 1871 with his wife and nine children. The two eldest sons were now following their father's trade.

In 1875—the year the Frys moved to Picked Stones—the Kerslake family also left Simonsbath, and William Hodge, a son of Thomas Hodge, who was one of the carpenters listed on the Census of 1851, returned to the village where he spent his boyhood, and set up in business there as a wheelwright and carpenter.

According to John Kerslake's obituary, published in the *North Devon Journal* 2.2.1905, he was associated with the Methodist Church for most of his life and was for many years a lay preacher. When he first arrived at Simonsbath from North Molton he found himself practically shut away from Methodism; the nearest Chapel being five miles away. At that time there was no evening service of any kind in the village, so he opened his house for religious worship.

Higher Stables (now a Toilet Block) with White Rock Cottage and Schoolroom beyond.

White Rock Cottage.

School and Schoolhouse.

Simonsbath Bridge C.1910.

The three families living in the White Rock cottage complex when the Rev. Thornton first came to Simonsbath in 1856, were reduced to two at the time of the 1861 Census. Only one of the cottages was listed as White Rock, and living there was John Steer, the eldest son of Joseph Steer, who we will come to shortly. It is not unlikely that John Steer had been living in this cottage since 1855, when he married Temperance Square at Exford, and it was here they raised eight of their nine children, the first having died in infancy; and here John remained until his death in 1892.

John Steer, a labourer, did not, as suggested in my first book, rent the White Rock smallholding, but did for a couple of years after his father's death, rent his farm, hence the confusion.

In the adjoining cottage—listed simply as 'Simonsbath' in 1861—on to which the school was built in 1857, lived John H. Cullen, a civil engineer, and his daughter Anne who was the schoolteacher. John H. Cullen is a man of some interest because it was he who was employed by Frederic Knight to survey and construct a railway from Simonsbath to Porlock Weir to solve the pressing problem of getting the iron ore from the mines on Exmoor to the coast for shipment to South Wales, for which Dowlais were obliged under the terms of their agreement to supply the rails and other ironwork; and the other two companies to contribute to the cost of its construction.

Unfortunately, by the time the project was finally got under way, two of the three mining companies had left the Moor, and with a depression in the iron trade, coupled with the inability to find commercially viable quantities of iron ore, Dowlais were no longer convinced that a railway to the coast was such a good idea. Nevertheless, Frederic Knight pressed ahead with his plans, and under the heading 'Exmoor Railway' John Cullen placed an advertisement in the *North Devon Journal* (6.12.1860) offering one or two pupils, on moderate terms, an extensive and practical knowledge of engineering, surveying, use of instruments and mechanical drawings. The address given for replies was Exmoor Railway, Larkborough House, Simonsbath, South Molton, as this was where he had his office.

We do not know if any young men took up John Cullen's offer, but if they did, they—like their tutor—were not to see the railway project come to fruition. Dowlais refused to supply the rails, or to continue mining, preferring to pay Frederic Knight £7,000, with all the buildings and mining plant thrown in rather than continue with what they considered to be a lost cause. Shortly after, John Cullen—no doubt bemused and frustrated by all the wrangling—left Exmoor, taking his daughter with him.

The Rev. Thornton's successor as Vicar of Exmoor was the Rev. Morton Drummond who was 29 and single when he took the living in 1861. Within a couple of years he had married, and in 1864 a son, Edmund, was baptised, followed by daughters in 1865 and 66. Very little else is known about this man or his relationship with his parishioners, but he appears to have enjoyed such sport as the Moor and village had to offer, and on a number of occasions played—without distinction—for the Simonsbath cricket team against teams from some of the parishes around the Moor.

Although William Kingdom—the blacksmith—and his wife Catherine are not recorded on the Census of 1861, their son William was. He was now 22 years old and a blacksmith in his own right, but it would appear that because he was a single man, the cottage he had grown up in had been let to William Vellacott, who was listed on the census as a labourer and farmer of 85 acres. According to Kelly's Directory of the same year he was also the Parish Clerk. William Kingdom was a boarder in this household, as too was another blacksmith, John Bragg, aged 17, from North Molton.

Frederic Knight's Rent Roll for Lady Day 1864 reveals that William Vellacott was now living in one of the White Rock cottages and was running his farm from there.

From more than one source I have heard that in his younger days William Vellacott had been in charge of much of the wall and hedge building on the Exmoor Estate. This was probably in the 1840s when Frederic Knight was creating his new farms, and not—as has been suggested—at the time of the enclosure of the estate in the early 1820s, because William was not born until 1817.

William Vellacott gave up his cottage and farm at Michaelmas 1865 and moved on. In 1871 we find him living at Higher Prescott, in the Parish of Exford, but after his wife's death in 1875 he returned to Exmoor, though not to the village of Simonsbath, but just outside at Bale Water, where in 1881 he was working as a road contractor and farming a few acres. He remarried in December in the same year and died two years later.

William Kingdom, who regained possession of the family home in 1864 when William Vellacott moved to White Rock, was also renting the blacksmith shop, a garden and a meadow at this time, for which he was paying a total rent of £19.14.0. a year. In 1865 he also became the Parish Clerk.

By 1871, William Kingdom had married*, lost his wife in childbirth, and was left with an infant son to raise. At this time William's mother—Catherine—herself a widow, was keeping house for him, with the help of a young servant girl. Also living in was a second blacksmith, William Handford.

In 1875 William remarried. His second wife was none other than William Vellacott's daughter, Mary Elizabeth, with whom he was lodging in 1861. Five children were born to this marriage; four daughters and one son—Ernest John—who was destined to follow his father in the same cottage.

At some time between 1875 and 1881, William Kingdom succeeded William Shapland as sub-postmaster, and the Post Office was then moved from the cottage at the west end of the row of cottages above and at right angles to Pound Cottages, to the east end, and remained there until about 1922, when William's son Ernest gave it up to concentrate more fully on his farming interests.

Although there is still much to be written concerning the Kingdom family, we need to take our leave of them for the moment in order to complete our survey of the remainder of the inhabitants of the village of Simonsbath in 1861.

* 31.3.1869. William Kingdom m Elizabeth Fry—William Fry's Daughter.

Thomas Elworthy, recorded on the Census as a farmer, was living with his wife and three sons and a daughter in one of the 'Simonsbath' cottages, the standard address at this time—and later—for most of the villagers, but in this instance it has not been necessary to work out by a process of elimination where Thomas lived, because Kelly's Directory of the same date—and subsequent issues—all give his address as Lower House, which was the end cottage of the row of Pound Cottages—nearest the river.

It has been said that Thomas Elworthy helped with the construction of many of the farmhouses and buildings erected on the Exmoor Estate in the late 1840s. Maybe he did, but he was certainly not living on Exmoor at that time unless he was in temporary lodgings, and did not settle there until about 1853*, long after most of Frederic Knight's new farms had been completed and let.

The Rent Roll of 1864 tells us that Thomas Elworthy was renting 120 acres of land at a rental of £50.5.0. a year. 60 acres of this land had been taken out of the old Deer Park and enclosed by Thomas, and though he had given it up by 1867, it is still known locally as Elworthy's Allotment.

According to the Census of 1861, Joseph Steer lived next door to Thomas Elworthy, and Mrs Ivy Tucker—née Steer—of Exford, has confirmed that her grandfather Richard Steer—Joseph's youngest son—was living in the same cottage in the 1890s. Lower House and Joseph Steer's cottage were at one time known as South and North Lower House, but in the 1970s were amalgamated to form one dwelling house, known as Pound Cottage.

Joseph Steer, the father of nine children, all—apart from his eldest son John of White Rock—born on Exmoor, was for many years employed by John Knight—and later his son—as a ploughman, walking endless miles behind his team of horses or oxen. He was living on Exmoor at least as early as 1835, and the Census of 1841 places him in one of the Limecombe Cottages. By 1851 he was living at Bale Water, where he remained for a few more years before settling in Simonsbath around 1858, to begin farming the 22 acres of land he is credited with in the Rent Roll of 1864, for which he was paying £13.16.6. a year.

For many years before the Church was built in Simonsbath, Joseph used to drive the Knight family servants to church on Sundays, either to Exford—the nearest—or possibly Brendon, where John Knight, and later his son Frederic, were patrons of the living. For these duties Joseph was paid 2s.1d. each Sunday.

It was the positive identification of Thomas Elworthy living at Lower House, with Joseph Steer next door that provided the key to the whereabouts of the Simonsbath Inn-cum-Refreshment House. In the 1861 Census, John Hasking of Simonsbath Inn is listed after Joseph Steer and Thomas Elworthy. In 1871 James Fry's Refreshment House (the inn) is placed between Thomas Elworthy and Joseph Steer, but even though they are not listed in quite the same order in 1871 there is no reason to doubt that they are all part of the

* A daughter born at Twitchen in 1852. A son born Exmoor Dec. 1853.

same block, and that the Inn-cum-Refreshment House was at that date at the higher end of the Pound Cottages row.

There does not appear to have been any intention on Frederic Knight's part to relet Simonsbath House following the departure of Mr and Mrs Torr in 1860, and when the half yearly Rent Audit was held at the Red Deer Inn on the Exford Road in September of the same year, it was reported in the *North Devon Journal* that there was the prospect of Mr and Mrs Knight taking up residence at Simonsbath at some time during the Parliamentary recess. The old house was not let again in their lifetime, even though for much of the year the only inhabitants to be found there were the caretaker and occasional servant. This was the case in 1861, when we find only Samuel Horwood, a gardener, and his daughter Susan, the housekeeper, living there.

Samuel Horwood was yet another of John Knight's early employees, listed as a leveller in the Labour Accounts of 1835 and 36. For many years he lived in one of the old Warren Cottages (now in ruins) below the farm, before moving to Simonsbath, first into the cottage where John Steer was now living and then into Simonsbath House.

It is by no means clear where the next family to appear in the Census of 1861—that of Isaac Bawden—lived, but on reflection it seems likely that this family was in temporary accommodation in part of Simonsbath House, because when they left the village shortly after, they left no gap to fill.

Frederic Knight's Rent Roll for Lady Day 1864, reveals that Isaac Bawden was renting Cloven Rocks Cottage and some land at this time, for which he was paying £16. a year. It is not unlikely that this cottage was being refurbished and gotten ready for him in 1861, because there is no mention of it in the Census, even though it was one of the earliest cottages built on Exmoor.

Isaac Bawden was one of four constables on Exmoor in 1862, the others being William Fry, John Kerslake and Thomas Elworthy, but in the early part of 1865, although he had paid his rent to Lady Day, Isaac had given up Cloven Rocks Cottage and the land he had been renting, and had left Exmoor.

The three cottages now known as Nos 4, 5 and 6 West Cottages, standing alongside the Challacombe road, about a quarter of a mile from the centre of the village of Simonsbath, were recorded as 'New Cottages' in the Census of 1861 and 1871, at which time there were but two cottages by a different arrangement. Richard Rook, a labourer, lived in the cottage furthest from the village; John Smith, a mason and builder in Frederic Knight's employ, lived in the other. There is a remarkable similarity in the design of these cottages, and those built for the miners at Cornham Ford, which is not really surprising, seeing as how they were built at around the same time.

At some time between 1861 and 1871, Richard Rook—who married Joseph Steer's daughter Matilda in 1854—moved into the cottage formerly held by Robert Holcombe; not the inn, but the cottage in between those inhabited by William Shapland and William Kingdom. How long Richard remained there is not known, but by 1881 he and his family were gone from the Moor.

John Smith the builder and his wife were still living in the other New Cottage in 1871, by which time William Tucker, a gamekeeper from Braunton, now working for Frederic Knight, was living next door.

The last house recorded on the Census of 1861 within the village, was Simonsbath Barton, a farm of just over 600 acres, which since 1854 had been in the tenancy of George Avery Gould at a rental of £247 a year. At this time he was employing four labourers—his two sons being still at school.

A report in the *North Devon Journal* (7.4.1859) tells us that George Gould had cause to take action against one of his employees, Samuel Harris. The case was heard at the Taunton Assizes, where Harris was accused of stealing six pecks of wheat and other articles from his employer. He was found guilty of all the charges against him, and because of previous convictions was given twelve months imprisonment with hard labour.

Although George Gould lived at the Barton for 14 years very little else is known about him or his family during the time they lived there, apart from one further item recorded in the North Devon Journal (18.1.1865), when John Steer, a blacksmith of Exford, took action against him at the South Molton Court for the recovery of a debt of £1.10.6. for smithying goods supplied. Gould did not bother to appear, and a Court order was issued for the immediate payment of the debt. Three years later George Gould gave up the Barton and left Exmoor.

That the 1850s and 60s were momentous years as far as the history of Simonsbath is concerned there is no doubt. The establishment of a church and school, together with an inn, bakehouse, shop and post office had turned it into a village in its true sense, but without the settlement there of the right kind of families all this would have counted for nothing. This was particularly true in a moorland village as remote as Simonsbath, which, in bad winters, was often cut off from the outside world for weeks at a time, when, had the inhabitants not all pulled together, many of them would not have survived.

The change of policy implemented by Frederic Knight in regard to letting as much land on his Exmoor Estate as was possible, certainly paid dividends where his own former employees were concerned, not only in the rents he received, but in kind, for these were the men who formed the backbone of the community within the village of Simonsbath, and continued to do so for many years.

CHAPTER 6

SIMONSBATH IN THE LATE 19TH CENTURY

NOW THAT Simonsbath had become a true village with a more settled community, it became possible for the villagers to organise their lives a little better. Most of the villagers became keen gardeners—they had to be—but few of the gardens adjoined their cottages, a point we will deal with more fully later, and though in Simonsbath—because of its height above sea level—crops were a little later, they were equal in quality and quantity to anything grown at a lower level in villages around the Moor.

In the early 1870s, following the improvement in school education, nearly every village in the country set up its own Reading Room, where for a small subscription members could come to read the daily papers and popular magazines of the time. There was usually also a small library to draw from, and though we do not know when the Reading Room at Simonsbath was built, we do know that it was situated at the top end of what is now Boevey's Restaurant. The same room is at present used as a store.

Hunting was—and still is—very much a part of the Exmoor scene, and most of the small farmers in the village in those days had an Exmoor pony or carthorse they would saddle up—or ride bareback if they had no saddle—and take off after the hunt whenever they were in the vicinity. It was by no means unusual for those without a horse to run miles on foot, just for a glimpse of the hounds in full cry after a deer or fox.

Cricket was also very much in vogue from the early 1860s on. Inter-village matches in the Exmoor region became commonplace, though only a few involving the Simonsbath team appear to have been recorded in local newspapers of the time. Two matches, both against Winsford, are worthy of note.

Although no mention has been found of the cricket match played against Winsford in the early part of the 1862 cricket season, the return match played at Simonsbath was recorded in the *North Devon Journal* (31.7.1862). On this occasion the Winsford team were well and truly beaten. They were all out for 9 runs in their first innings, with Thomas Elworthy—the son of farmer Tom—taking four wickets, and Robert Smith, the son of Robert of Emmetts Grange—also taking four. Simonsbath then set about building a respectable score. The team and their scorers are as follows: Rev. Drummond 4. T. Baker (Driver farm) 4; R. Smith jun. 1; R. Smith sen. 2; W. Steer (son of Joseph) 10; T. Elworthy 43; W. Kingdom 26; Thos. Scott (Winstitchen) 1; W. Vellacott 0; W. Elworthy (Thomas's brother) 1; W. Scott (Winstitchen) 0;—102 runs in all. The Rev. Anderson was Winsford's most successful bowler, taking 7 wickets. Winsford did a little better in their second innings but were still all out for 26 runs; far short of the number needed to force Simonsbath to play again.

In July of the following year, in a more evenly contested match held at the Vicarage, Winsford, the Exmoor team scored 55 and 61. In reply, Winsford scored 52 and 66 and won by just 2 runs.

A tragic accident—though not one involving a Simonsbath person—was recorded in the *North Devon Journal* (21.7.1864). It would appear that a young man named Gordon, the son of a clergyman from Ashton-Under-Lyne was on a walking tour in the West Country and on arriving at Simonsbath, and the day being hot, he decided to take a bathe in the River Barle at the spot known as Simonsbath Pool, which was about 15ft deep. His clothes were later found on the bank of the river and a search was initiated, ending with the discovery of his body at the bottom of the pool.

In the late 1860s, a depression in the farming industry brought about a further change in policy on the Exmoor Estate when some of the larger farms came in hand and proved impossible to relet. Frederic Knight quickly realised that in such circumstances the only way he could maintain his income was to stock the farms himself and this led to the re-introduction of Cheviot sheep, which were brought down from Scotland by Scottish shepherds, most of whom were persuaded to settle on Exmoor, although only one or two settled in Simonsbath itself, and then not for long.

Only one farmer in the village is known to have gone bankrupt at this time. He was John Baker, who had taken the White Rock smallholding in 1865, following the departure of William Vellacott. On Lady Day 1867, John paid his half yearly rent in full, but shortly after, appears to have run out of money and credit, and on the 29th June he was adjudged bankrupt at a County Court hearing at South Molton. The first meeting of his creditors was held in July and the usual notices placed in local newspapers requesting proof of money owed and debts due, but so little was forthcoming from his estate that Mr Crosse, the Registrar, felt it his duty to examine poor John Baker at great length at his final examination in September. He must have been satisifed that Baker—now living at Lynton—had no hidden assets, and an order of discharge from bankruptcy was granted, subject to the usual 30 days appeal.

Simonsbath Barton, given up by George Gould in 1868, was one of the few farms relet in this time of depression. The new tenants were the Red brothers from Culbone, although only one, William, appears to have lived at the Barton. They were paying £50 a year less than Gould, for the same acreage. The partnership lasted until 1875, and from that time on, until his death in 1911, William Red alone held the tenancy. He had lived at the Barton for 44 years, one of the longest tenancies held by the same man recorded on the Exmoor Estate. Sadly he lost his only son in 1900 at the age of only 34, but a daughter, who married William Gammin in 1912, continued to farm at the Barton until they retired in 1934 and went to live at Exford.

There was no further expansion to the village during the period 1861-1871, nor had there been many changes of occupants of the cottages therein, other than those already referred to. Once again Simonsbath House was unoccupied when the Census of 1871 was recorded, apart from a caretaker, but not

Samuel Horwood, who had passed on, or his daughter, but Mary Stoneman, a widow from North Molton. The only other resident there at this time was John Easman, a shepherd from Scotland, who had probably brought down a flock of sheep, and could well have been on the point of returning home as there is no mention of him thereafter.

Living in the Vicarage in 1871 was the Rev. W. H. Thompson, who had taken over from the Rev. Drummond, following his departure in 1868. In January, 1869, the new vicar gave what could be termed an inaugural supper for about 50 of his parishioners in the schoolroom, which according to a report in the *North Devon Journal*, was well decorated for the occasion. Patriotic and other toasts were drunk. The rest of the evening was given over to musical entertainment, and a good time was had by one and all.

Among the servants living in the vicarage in 1871 was William Elworthy, a groom, age 28, who was the second son of Thomas Elworthy of Lower House. Two years later, William married Frances, the eldest daughter of William Tucker—Frederic Knight's gamekeeper.

In September 1875, the Rev. Thompson took the tenancy of Cloven Rocks Cottage, along with two or three small fields and a large enclosure known as Higher Allotment, and shortly after, William Elworthy moved into the cottage. He was still living there in 1881 with his wife and family, now consisting of three sons and two daughters and was still employed by the Rev. Thompson, but as a gardener, not a groom; this position having been taken by his brother-in-law Alfred Tucker.

In 1883, the Rev. Thompson gave up almost all the land he had been renting on the Exmoor Estate, retaining only one small meadow and Cloven Rocks Cottage, where William Elworthy and his family continued to live until 1890. In the following year when the Census was recorded, they were again living in the Vicarage.

Shortly before the Rev. Thompson gave up his rented land on Exmoor, he purchased Dennington House, Swimbridge, along with the adjoining Barton Farm. An advertisement in the *North Devon Journal* dated 21.6.1883, in regards to the letting of Dennington Barton, reveals that Alfred Tucker, former groom to the Vicar, but now his gardener, was living in Dennington House and would show prospective tenants around the farm. It is thought that the Rev. Thompson remained at Simonsbath until his retirement in 1892, but he was not recorded at either place when the Census of 1891 was taken.*

That the Rev. Thompson had a deep affection for his parishioners—and they for him—there is no doubt, and shortly after the wedding of his youngest daughter, Rose Edith, to the Rev. John Frederick Chanter of Parracombe in June 1889, the Vicar and his wife invited all the inhabitants of the parish of Exmoor to a treat in honour of the young couple on their return from honeymoon.

The event was described in the *North Devon Journal* of 15.8.1889 as a

* He was in fact living at Ilfracombe when the 1891 Census was taken.

'Red Letter Day' in the history of the picturesque moorland village of Simonsbath, and so indeed it was, such treats being very few and far between.

The day was exceptionally fine, the first for some time, and the rich dark foliage of the fir trees was enlivened by the bright colours of many flags. First the children were provided with tea in the field near the hotel and then amused with games and races for prizes. In the field was a large marquee, which, however, had to be lengthened to accommodate all the visitors. In the marquee a cold collation of old English fare was spread, and although seats were provided for 150, they had to make room for another batch.

Having regaled themselves all round, the toast list was opened by the Rev. Thompson, proposing 'The Queen and Royal Family', with the band playing *God Save the Queen*. The next toast, proposed by William Brian—the Exmoor Estate Bailiff—was to the Rev. Thompson and Mrs Thompson, and with musical harmony the band played *For He's a Jolly Good Fellow*. Other toasts were drunk to the Rev. Chanter and Mrs Chanter, and to Sir Frederic Knight, with the band playing *Home Sweet Home* and *A Fine Old English Gentleman* respectively. The last toast was to the helpers.

The tables were then cleared and the marquee illuminated with Chinese Lanterns, and a programme of song and dance was then gone through; the music being supplied by the Parracombe Brass Band, under the direction of Mr A. Brown. Mr Fry of the hotel lent his piano for the occasion and this was most skilfully played by Miss Beadon. Among the songs were *What an Alteration*, sung by Mr Kingdom; *Sunshine and Rain*, Mrs Roope; *They all like Jack*, Mr Brian; *Last Night*, Mrs Chanter; *Bell of the Ball*, Mr J. Red; *Wonderful*, Rev. Chanter; *Fiddle and I*, Mrs Williams; *Eighteen Pence*, Mr W. Jennings and *Old Kentucky*, Mrs Williams, with banjo accompaniment. The cheering at the close for those who had provided such an enjoyable time showed how much it was appreciated. It was indeed a memorable day.

Three years later, at the age of 60, the Rev. Thompson took his leave of the good people of Exmoor. In the same year (1892) William Elworthy and most of his family moved from the Vicarage to Dennington, Swimbridge, where William was promoted from his former position as gardener to that of Farm Bailiff of what had now become an 800 acre estate.

The Rev. Thompson died in 1908 at the age of 76. His obituary (*North Devon Journal* 19.3.1908) tells us that besides having a wide practical knowledge of agriculture, he was also keenly interested in sport, and was an acknowledged expert on trout fishing. He was a man of fine physique, standing over 6ft tall, with a most genial disposition, beloved by a wide circle of friends. He was interred in Swimbridge churchyard, in the grave of his wife who predeceased him 12 years earlier. Of the six employees who were the bearers, four were from the Elworthy family.

The Rev. Thompson's successor at Simonsbath was the Rev. Pigot, a son of Preb. Pigot of Fremington. The induction took place in October 1893, in the presence of nearly all the inhabitants of the large and scattered parish of Exmoor. After the service the parishioners were entertained to tea in the schoolroom. The rest of the evening was given over to dancing to the strains of a violin played by Mr Taylor of Lynton.* Two years later, for the first time in history, a confirmation service was held at Simonsbath, with 30 confirmed, 18 males and 12 females.

It is not perhaps surprising that there were frequent changes of teachers at Simonsbath School during the first 40 years of its existence, when we consider the isolation of the place in those days and that many of the teachers were young single women who probably had no idea what they were letting themselves in for, but come they did, remaining there for about five years on average, and then moving on again.

With the departure of John Cullen and his schoolteacher daughter Annie, who for a few years after the Rev. Thornton and his assistant teacher Miss Emma Reed left Exmoor, taught at the school, there was again a vacancy for a teacher. The next schoolmistress appears to have been a Miss Louisa Brazier, who according to Kelly's Directory of 1866, was resident at that time. She had moved on by 1871, at which time we find William Richards—a shoemaker—and his wife Sarah, the schoolmistress, living in the schoolhouse. At some time before 1875, they too had left the village, because on the 4th of January in that year Annie Blackmore, the daughter of a Customs Officer, William Blackmore, is recorded as the schoolteacher at Simonsbath, when she married Thomas Scott, a shepherd, the son of William Scott, the Exmoor Estate Bailiff at that time. How much longer Thomas Scott and his wife remained on Exmoor is uncertain but by 1876 he had been replaced as a shepherd and it seems likely that they left the Moor at this time.

Mrs Scott's father, William Blackmore, may or may not have been the Customs Officer who was led a merry dance by a moorland character who went by the name of Fiddle de Dee, who, according to a recent phone call from a Mr Hammett, used to drink regularly at the old Acland Arms Inn at Moles Chamber.* When Fiddle de Dee's wife considered he had spent enough time and money at the inn she used to go there to fetch him; he chasing her all the way home.

It is not known at what date this occurred but it would have been before 1883, because the licence of the inn was given up in that year. Nor do we know where Fiddle de Dee lived. Mrs Margaret Prout of Rose Cottage, Simonsbath, vaguely remembers her father (Jack Little) talking about him when she was a young girl, but that is not to say he lived in Simonsbath, or even on Exmoor Proper.

On one occasion when a Customs Officer called at the Acland Arms, Fiddle de Dee asked him if a licence was needed for fancy dogs, and on being told it was, said to the Customs man, 'In that case you had better come with me as my wife has a couple of fancy dogs and she has no licence for them'. Off they went over the Moor and eventually arrived at his home, where he

---

* *North Devon Journal* 5.10.1893.

* Mr Hammett's source of information was George Smith—or Smyth—(to whom he was related by marraige), a son of Jeremiah Smyth, the landlord of the inn for many years.

gleefully pointed to two ornamental china dogs on the mantlepiece above the fireplace and said 'There's my wife's fancy dogs'. The Customs Officer's reply is not known, and if it was, would no doubt be unprintable.

Living in the schoolhouse in 1881 was Harriet Carpenter, a widowed dressmaker, and her daughter Zena, who was the schoolteacher. They had been there at least three years because in March 1878—according to the *North Devon Journal*—George Norman, a butcher of Simonsbath (probably Horsen Farm) put in a successful claim at South Molton Court for payment for meat supplied to Miss Zena Carpenter. She was ordered to pay 3s.6d.

By 1883 the Carpenters were gone from Simonsbath and we find a Miss Mary Webster installed in the schoolhouse. She in turn had been replaced before 1889 by Mrs Ellen Buttercase, a widow, with a young son Robert. She was still living in the schoolhouse in 1891, which she had named Primrose Cottage, but shortly after gave in her notice and left for Canada.*

The next teacher at the school was Miss Octavia Smyth, who had moved on by 1897, when we find Mrs W. J. Nichols in charge at the school, and having now come to the end of the period covered by this chapter we will take our leave of the school in order to bring the rest of the village and its inhabitants up to date.

If there were frequent changes of occupant at the schoolhouse, the same cannot be said of one of the two cottages adjoining it, where—as already noted—John Steer had lived for nearly 40 years until his death in 1892, only three years after the tragic death of his only son—also John—at the age of only 29.

John Steer junior, employed by Sir Frederic Knight as a carter, had been sent to South Molton station with his horses and a wagon to fetch a load of corn. He did not return at the expected time, and later his father set off to see what had become of him and was shocked to find him lying dead near his horses and wagon along the stretch of road known as Emmetts Plain. The body was cold and his father estimated he had been dead 2½ to 3 hours. There was slight bruising to his face and shoulder, but nothing to indicate the cause of death. A verdict of 'Found Dead' was recorded.*

The other cottage in the White Rock complex had, since the bankruptcy of John Baker in 1867, been given over to William Red of Simonsbath Barton, to house one of his labourers. In 1871 this was Thomas Dowding and his family, who had his father—now a widower—living with him. In the same year they moved into one of the Limecombe Cottages, and though the Census of 1881 gives a John Sanders[§] living in the old cottage, there may well have been other occupants in between, because according to the school admission registers, the Sanders family had only just arrived in the village from Heasley Mill. By 1891 they were gone from Exmoor and Fred Wyburn[§] was living there.

---

* *North Devon Journal* 10.9.1891.
* *North Devon Journal* 6.5.1889.
[§] Both men married daughters of John Steer.

In the last chapter we briefly mentioned James Fry, who took over the Simonsbath Inn-cum-Refreshment House, bakehouse, shop and land—formerly rented by Robert Holcombe—in 1865 at a rental of £46 p.a. According to Frederic Knight's Rent Roll of 1866, James Fry was in partnership with a John Smyth, who was probably closely related to Mrs Fry (née Smyth), but as he is not to be found in any of the later Census Returns for Exmoor it is to be presumed that he was a sleeping partner.

In 1870, eight years after the licence of the Simonsbath Inn had been given up, James Fry applied for—and was granted—a wine licence for his Refreshment House. The Census of 1871 does not suggest it was a large establishment, and apart from James and his wife the only other people living there were a 5-year-old niece and a young domestic servant. In the following year—some eight years after their marraige—their only child, Edith, was born.

When William Fry gave up Ashcombe Farm in 1875 and moved out of the village to Picked Stones Farm, James Fry took over his former house and farm buildings, along with 112 acres of his best land, while still retaining the Refreshment House and other premises, and the land he had been renting since 1865. He was now paying a combined rent of £200 a year.

In the updated version of *The Reclamation of Exmoor Forest* published in 1970—but not in the first edition—R. J. Sellick vaguely refers to additions to the old Simonsbath Inn (Refreshment House) in 1878, with James Fry hauling the materials used. It is now believed it was not the old inn that was enlarged, but the house he had taken over from William Fry, and this then became the Refreshment House, and much later—the Exmoor Forest Hotel. So much for the claim made by a former proprietor of the hotel a few years ago that the inn was of 17thC origin, and even if it had still been on its former site, would not date earlier than 1820. Similar claims had been made in respect of the Sportsmans Inn at Sandyway, and the Crown Hotel Exford, both of which date from the first half of the 19th Century.

The Census of 1881 lists James Fry as the keeper of a refreshment house and farmer of 170 acres. The Refreshment House had not yet become the prosperous concern it was to be later. Only two servants were employed at this time; one a young female domestic; the other a farm lad—both living in.

James Fry is listed twice in Kelly's Directory of 1883, first as the proprietor of a first class Refreshment House, within 10 miles of Lynton, with apartments for families and tourists, with free fishing for visitors staying there. Secondly he is described as a grocer and farmer, which suggests that though he may have transferred part of his business to new premises, the grocers shop remained where it was, and as his former Refreshment House does not appear in any shape or form in either the Census of 1881 or 1891 it had probably been converted to some other use.

In 1880, the first of what was to become an annual auction of livestock for the yeomen of the district was held at Simonsbath in the field adjoining Mr Fry's private hotel, with dinner served on the premises. A report on the auction held there two years later by Messrs Sanders and Son the auctioneers, describes it as a more important sale than last year with excellent prices being obtained.* The auctions continued to be held in the same field until 1885, but in the following year it was transferred to the Barton, although dinner was still served at the hotel.

In 1887, probably in commemoration of Queen Victoria's Golden Jubilee, James Fry changed the name of the Refreshment House to that of one of the Queen's forebears—William Rufus—who, according to legend, afforested Exmoor some 700 years before. We will come to the Simonsbath celebration of this great occasion shortly, but in the meantime let us continue with James Fry's story.

A report in the *North Devon Journal* (6.2.1879) of a Court case held at Barnstaple in the previous week, reveals that James Fry of Simonsbath was summoned by the Barnstaple Union to support his father, James Fry senior of Stoke Rivers, who for the past four years had been receiving 6/- a week in outside relief. A similar summons was issued to another son, Thomas Fry, formerly of Ilfracombe but now of London.

Both men had been to see their father within the past few weeks on learning that he had become too ill to work, to see if he needed any financial help for his support. Their father assured them that he did not. As the case evolved it became clear that two other sons were paying 3/- a week each towards their father's upkeep and that one of them, Henry, with whom their father was living, had, without his authorisation gone behind his back to the Barnstaple Union and obtained 6/- a week outside relief. The outcome of the case was that each son should contribute 1s.6d. a week to support their father, and that James and Thomas Fry should pay part of the costs of the Court action against them. James Fry paid his share, but his brother said that although he was willing to pay 1s.6d. a week towards his father's support, he had no intention of paying any of the Court's costs.

Kelly's Directory of 1889, and the Census of 1891, indicate that the William Rufus had now become a flourishing hotel. The former reveals that it was also a 'posting house' with hunters available for hire. The latter tells us that James Fry was employing a full time waitress and two general domestic servants, and two farm servants, all living in.

Two of the staff, Ann M. Watts, the waitress age 18, and Bertram Watts age 13, one of the farm servants, were sister and brother to Harry Watts, who for many years farmed in and around Simonsbath. According to Mrs Anne Buckingham—Harry's daughter, who was born in Simonsbath—her father also worked for James Fry as a young man, but at a later date. He described him as a hard taskmaster. By the time James retired in 1900, he had become a wealthy man.

Joseph Steer, who for 20 years or so farmed a few acres from one of the Pound Cottages, died in 1880 age 77. For a short time after his death, his eldest son John of White Rock Cottage, rented his father's farm, but on

Lady Day 1883, his younger brother William took over the farm, remaining where he was, with his mother, in the family home.

William, who never married, had, like his father before him, worked for many years on the Exmoor Estate. In 1876, when steam ploughing was introduced following successful trials three years earlier, William became the driver of the steam ploughing engine, and many acres of hitherto unbroken moorland were ploughed in this way.

In September 1883, shortly after he had taken over the family farm, William Steer increased the size of his holding by taking 12 acres of the land which had been recently given up by the Rev. Thompson. He continued to work the farm until his death in 1893, only a year after that of his brother John.

The next tenant of the farm was Richard Steer—William and John's younger brother—who had been shepherd in charge of the Simonsbath Herding since 1888, at which time he and his family moved from Cornham— where he had formerly worked as a labourer—into the family home with William. After his brother's death, Richard gave up his sheep herding and took on the farm. He was the last of the Steer family to live in Pound Cottage—sometimes known as North Lower House—because owing to a weak chest, which was not helped by the close proximity of the cottage to Ashcombe Water and the River Barle, Richard was allowed to move into one of the two new cottages known as Jubilee Cottages which were built in 1897, and continued to run his farm from there until his death in 1906.

When we took our leave of William Kingdom in the last chapter he had just taken over the Post Office from William Shapland, and was combining his duties as sub-postmaster with his business as a blacksmith and farmer, and had, since 1865, also been the Parish Clerk. Shortly afterwards, he was appointed Relieving School Attendance Officer, and in 1886 became Registrar of Births and Deaths for the Exmoor District.

When William Kingdom took over the Post Office, deliveries of letters were still restricted to three days a week, but by 1883 were arriving daily at 11.10am, with the outgoing mail leaving at 2.30pm. During recent further research on the *North Devon Journals*, the name and sad demise of the postman delivering letters to the Post Office at Simonsbath has come to light. He was John Frayne Westcott, whose death and obituary were recorded in the *North Devon Journal* on 3.5.1894, the gist of which is as follows.

"There is much gloom in North Molton on hearing of the death of the Heasley Mill and Simonsbath postman, John Frayne Westcott of North Molton, who was found dead in a field on Emmetts Grange Farm, Exmoor. The lately deceased was subject to epileptic fits which had slightly interfered with his duties. On Friday morning he left North Molton at his usual time apparently in good health, but before reaching Fyldon he was seized of a fit and fell from his pony, cutting his head. He was taken to a house close by and his injuries attended to, and advised to go home, but as he now felt much better he decided to resume his journey. When he reached Emmetts Grange he tied his pony to the hedge inside the field and walked to the house

The Old Post Office, about 1900. Group L. to R. Ernest Kingdom, Hettie Kingdom, N.K. and Harry Watts.

Pitt Cottage and Old Post Office from Ashcombe Water, about 1900.

Mr. & Mrs. William Kingdom of Cornham Farm and Mrs. Kingdoms mother (seated), Jack Lock and Francey Coward.

Lower House and Smithy. Group L. to R. Ernest Kingdom, Jack Elworthy, child N.K. and Hettie Kingdom.

about half a mile from the road, delivered his letters and went away. On returning to his pony he took a short cut across the field and must have been seized with another fit and expired. Later in the day, with the mail several hours overdue, the Postmaster at Simonsbath (William Kingdom) set out to meet him and found his body where stated. The body was cold and had been dead about five hours when found at 3.30pm. The deceased had been a postman in the district for about 22 years and had only recently taken to riding his pony during the journey. He was the oldest member of the North Molton Church Choir and was highly respected by everyone who knew him. Much sympathy was expressed to the widow and children.''

As the years passed, the gap between delivery of the mail and departure widened until by 1906 it was arriving at Simonsbath at 9.30am and leaving again at 2.30pm. At some time after 1888 a small hut was built on the opposite side of the road from what is now the Simonsbath Pottery, to accommodate the postman during the long hours he had to remain there before it was time to return. This hut and a lean-to shed at the rear to house the postman's pony and trap are still remembered by one or two of Simonsbath's older inhabitants—when the mail was coming from South Molton in the early years of this century. The hut was simply furnished with a couch and small stove, but quite comfortable. In 1923, when deliveries of mail were switched from South Molton to Barnstaple and were made by motor van, this vehicle too was housed in the shed formerly occupied by the pony and trap, and it was not until the early 1930s, when deliveries of mail began to arrive from Minehead via Exford Post Office—as it does today— that this shed and the postman's hut went out of use.

Strangely, although Simonsbath had had a Post Office for many years it was not until around the late 1880s that it became possible to obtain a postal order, and even then, none received by the villagers could be cashed there. The nearest post office for such transactions at that time was at North Molton, and after 1894—Exford. The same facilities were not available in Simonsbath until some time between 1906 and 1910. In following the history of Simonsbath Post Office we have gone far ahead of other changes taking place within the village, and it is now time to turn back the pages to pick up the threads once more.

In or around the year 1876, a new smithy was built on the south side of the Challacombe road—almost opposite the 'New Cottages' where William Tucker and John Smith were living in 1871—to enable running repairs to be carried out on Frederic Knight's steam ploughing engine and tackle, which he had recently acquired following successful trials three years earlier. At the same time, a second building was erected on the north side of the road to house the steam engine and tackle when not in use, and onto the east end of this building a new cottage was also built. This cottage was for many years afterwards the home of the Exmoor Estate Farm Bailiff, who at this date was William Brian who had replaced William Scott, following the latter's death in 1875.

It would appear that as no other blacksmith was resident in Simonsbath at this time, that it was William Kingdom who carried out the repairs to the ploughing machinery, but it is not known if he kept his old smithy open; possibly not, as he no longer employed a second blacksmith.

In the autumn of 1992, during renovations to the cottage and engine house next door—which was converted to two more cottages around the turn of the century—the plaster was ripped from the walls, revealing not one archway as expected, where the steam engine would have entered, but two. It would, therefore, appear that it was Frederic Knight's original intention to purchase two steam engines to work his ploughing tackle, one at each end of the field as was common at that time, but on finding that the same results could be achieved with a single engine placed at one end and an anchored pulley wheel at the other, only one engine, a 10 h.p. Amies Barford was used.

The two 'New Cottages' where William Tucker, the Exmoor Estate game-keeper, and John Smith, builder, had been living in 1871, had by 1881 become three cottages by a different arrangement, and were now known as West Cottages. William Tucker was still living in the cottage furthest from the village (No. 1) Frederick Blackmore, Frederic Knight's groom was living in No. 2 and George Huxtable, a farm labourer in No. 3. The cottage in which William Brian, the Exmoor Estate Bailiff was living, was now known as No. 4 West Cottages.

Frederick Blackmore had been living on Exmoor since the early 1860s. The Exmoor Estate Rent Roll of 1864 lists him as renting a cottage in Simonsbath—not specified—along with land, late Le Blanc's, and a meadow below Simonsbath House, for which he was paying £27 a year in rent. The cottage in Simonsbath was given up in 1869 and the land shortly after, and it was probably at this time that he moved to Duredon where for a few years he was employed as a shepherd on the estate before moving to West Cottages.

In the early part of 1879 Frederic Knight lost his only son. His obituary appeared in the *North Devon Journal* of 6.3.1879 and reads as follows:

'A very heavy affliction has fallen on F. W. Knight, Esq., the owner of Exmoor, M.P. for West Worcestershire and Mrs Knight on the death of their only son Frederic Sebright Winn Knight, Deputy Lieutenant and Justice of the Peace of the Counties of Devon and Somerset who died of the decline after a short illness at Simonsbath Lodge (House) on Friday last, the 28th February at the age of only 27. He was a gentleman of excellent parts and occasionally took his place at the Petty Sessions at Combe Martin and Dulverton. Much sympathy is felt for the bereaved parents under their irreplaceable loss.'

With no son to take over when he passed on, Frederic Knight is understand-ably said to have lost heart where his future plans for his beloved Exmoor Estate was concerned. He was now approaching 70 years of age, and with his property mortgaged to the tune of £123,060 it appears likely he could see little point in spending the remaining years of his life burdened with crippling mortgage repayments, and a capital debt he could not hope to repay without selling off the bulk of his estate, but hopeful that it could be kept in the family it was offered to his nearest relatives, who, after giving the matter some serious thought, declined his offer.

The Exmoor and Brendon Estates were then placed in Agent's hands, and a firm offer was made for the property, but on making inquiries into the identity of the would-be purchasers, with no names forthcoming, Frederic Knight reasoned that his estates could well be passing into the hands of unscrupulous speculators and refused to complete the transaction.

Frederic Knight retired from public life in 1885. In the following year he was knighted for services to the Yeomanry and Volunteer Movement, in which he held the rank of Colonel for many years. In the same year he sold the Reversion of the Exmoor and Brendon Estates to Lord Fortescue of Castle Hill, Filleigh for £190,060, which, after his mortgage was paid off, left him with considerably less capital than his father had paid for the two estates some 45 years earlier, before reclamation.

In 1887 church bells around the country rang out in celebration of Queen Victoria's Golden Jubilee. Cities, towns and villages throughout the country organised huge parties to celebrate the occasion. In Simonsbath the day chosen for their celebrations—according to a report in the *North Devon Journal* of 17.11.1887,—was the 46th birthday of the heir apparent. Sir Frederic Knight gave all the provisions for the occasion. Dinner was served, with a number of leading lights from the Exmoor area presiding over the tables. These included Sir Frederic and his Agent, Mr Smyth-Richards, and the Rev. Ayre; and from the village, William Red of Simonsbath Barton and James Fry of the William Rufus hotel.

At 6pm on the same day, tea was provided in the same room (the Wool Chamber), and at 8pm there was a grand display of fireworks, also given by Sir Frederic. The North Molton Brass Band were also in attendance. Tea was again provided on the following day for the women and children of the parish (compliments of Sir Frederic). A vote of thanks was given to Sir Frederic and his Lady for their great kindness, and toasts were proposed— and drunk—to 'long life and happiness to Her Majesty', and to Sir Frederic and his wife.

The Census of 1891 reveals that there had been little if any further development within the village during the past 10 years, and only a few changes of occupants therein. For the first time we find Sir Frederic and his wife in residence at Simonsbath House when a Census was recorded. There is little doubt that after he retired from a busy public life in 1885 they were able to spend much more time there than had hitherto been possible. Also in residence in the old house was Robert Jasper, who is described as a Sub-Bailiff, of whom we know nothing, and his wife, who was the current housekeeper of the establishment. To complete the complement of staff there was a housemaid, a ladies' maid and a footman, none of whom came from the North Devon-Exmoor area.

In 1892, Sir Frederic was fortunate to escape serious injury when he was involved in an alarming accident near his home. A report of the incident in the *North Devon Journal* (7.4.1891) states that he was driving a pair of horses towards the Moor, and on taking a sharp bend one of the traces became loose and got entangled in the horses legs, whereupon they bolted. Sir Frederic jumped from his carriage and fortunately sustained no personal injury. His coachman was not so lucky. He received ugly cuts to his head and body. The carriage was so badly damaged as to be unfit for further use.

Research into family history is never easy when successive generations of a family bear the same christian names. This was particularly true of the Elworthy family of Simonsbath, when at one time there were three generations of Thomas Elworthy's in the village, all renting land and cottages on the Exmoor Estate, and it was not until the recent release of the Census of 1891 that it became clear that the Thomas living at Lower House in that year was not the man of that name who took the tenancy of the cottage and small farm in the late 1850s, but his son Thomas Bale Elworthy, who for many years resided in the cottage at the abandoned Wheal Eliza Mine. It was in this cottage that Thomas and his wife Ann raised a large family; he working as a jobbing labourer and his wife taking in washing to help make ends meet. In fact we now know that Thomas took over his father's farm in 1886 following the latter's retirement to North Molton at the age of 73, where he died three years later.*

Only four of Thomas B. Elworthy's children—all sons—were still living at home at the time of the 1891 Census, and with their help a little more land was rented. By 1898 the eldest son—also Thomas—who married Eliza Watts of North Molton in 1894, was renting a cottage at Duredon and a little land, which by 1901 had been increased to 57 acres. In the same year, his brother William also began farming in a small way. He married Lucy Bond in 1906 and three years later was able to take the tenancy of Winstitchen Farm.

In June 1910 Thomas Bale Elworthy paid his last rent for Lower House and his smallholding, and in December of the same year his second son, John, (Jack) who in 1906 married Mary Watts—sister to the wife of his brother Thomas—took over the farm.

On giving up his farm Thomas B. Elworthy moved to Winstitchen where he rented a cottage adjacent to his son William's farmhouse. He remained there until his death in 1924 at the age of 85—eleven years aftrer the death of his wife Ann.

At some time around 1893, William Hodge, carpenter and wheelwright of Simonsbath, retired, but appears to have lived in the village for a few more years though he did not die there. If—as Census Returns indicate—his cottage adjoined the William Rufus Hotel, then there is every reason to believe that this cottage was incorporated with the hotel, and was the later addition referred to by R. J. Sellick in *The Reclamation of Exmoor Forest*. Certainly James Welch, who succeeded William Hodge as carpenter in Simonsbath, never lived in this cottage.

According to the Electoral Roll of 1893, James Welch was living in one of the West Cottages, probably that of Frederick Blackmore, whose address

---

* Information supplied by Colin Elworthy of Bickle Farm, Swimbridge.

was now given as Simonsbath, not West Cottages as formerly. How long James lived in this cottage is uncertain, but when one of his children went down with diphtheria in January, 1898 he was living in the caretaker's quarters in Simonsbath House.* He is also known to have lived in the cottage at Wheal Eliza Mine, but not when.

On the 3rd May, 1897, in his 85th year, Sir Frederic Knight died at Bath. Four days later his body was interred in the little churchyard at Simonsbath, at the very heart of his beloved kingdom of Exmoor. In the following week his obituary appeared in the *North Devon Journal*:

'Colonel Sir Frederic Winn Knight of Exmoor and Wolverley, Worcestershire, who represented West Worcs. for 44 years as a Conservative MP died last week at the age of 84. He was the eldest son of John Knight of Wolverley by his second wife, the elder daughter of the 1st Lord Headley, and a descendant of Richard Knight of Madely, Shropshire, a considerable iron master in the time of the Commonwealth. He was born in 1812 and was educated at Charterhouse. He was a Deputy Lieutenant and Magistrate of Worcs. and a Magistrate for Devon and Somerset. A family trustee of the British Museum as representative of the late R. Payne Knight of Downton. He served for many years in the local Yeomanry and Volunteers. He was married in 1850 to a daughter of the late Mr E. Gibbs and was created a K.C.B. in 1886. In 1841 the deceased was elected for West Worcs. and continued to represent the constituency until the passing of the Redistribution Act of 1885, when he retired from public life. In 1852, and again in 1858-9 he was Parliamentary Secretary to the Poor Law Board under Lord Derby's Government having in his early parliamentary days been a supporter of agricultural protection. The interment took place on Friday last. In addition to the members of his own family and the tenants of the deceased, the funeral was attended by Lord Ebrington, Mr Snow (Oare Manor), Mr R. S. Crosse of South Molton, Mr Smyth Richards of Barnstaple and others. The day being rough and the place inaccessible naturally reduced the numbers of those who would otherwise have attended.'

There was no large sale of live and dead stock following Sir Frederic Knight's death, as this was taken over at valuation by Viscount Ebrington—Lord Fortescue's son and heir—but there was a smaller sale on the 23rd July in the same year of some of the contents of Simonsbath House. The only livestock on offer was six choice pigs and a quantity of poultry.

On the day prior to the sale Lady Knight removed an old lock from one of the doors of the old house—this lock having originally been brought either from Wolverley or Sir Frederic's London home* and was of great sentimental value to Lady Knight—but before she left a new lock was fitted, and with this final symbolic gesture she was gone from Exmoor.

According to a copy of Sir Frederic Knight's Will, published in the *North Devon Journal* on 22.7.1897, he left a personal estate of £106,612, which although still a considerable fortune at that time was about £1000 less than

* G. C. Smyth-Richards' Diaries.

the original cost of the Exmoor and Brendon Estates before any reclamation work was carried out, and certainly did not reflect the increased value of the Exmoor Estate following the enormous capital outlay on the reclamation and the creation of the village of Simonsbath and a number of large farms. Poor recompense indeed for the two men who had done so much to turn a desolate moorland into the prosperous farming community it had become at the time of Sir Frederic's death.

Sir Frederic left £1000 apiece to three of his five executors and £200 a year for life to his cousin Edward Frederic Knight. He also left £800 a year to his nephew Eric Ayshford Knight until the death of Lady Knight, whereupon her life interest in her husband's estate passed to him.

Three years after Sir Frederic's death Lady Knight was laid to rest beside him and their son. An era had ended, a new one begun.

CHAPTER 7

THE VILLAGE ENLARGED—
OLD FAMILIES—NEW ARRIVALS

WITH the death of Sir Frederic Knight, the Exmoor and Brendon Estates passed into the hands of Earl Fortescue of Castle Hill, Filleigh, who had purchased the Reversion 11 years earlier. On the 12th January 1898 he officially made them over to his eldest son and heir, Viscount Ebrington, who, since Sir Frederic's death, had been out and about the estates familiarising himself with the farms and the village of Simonsbath and making plans for its development.

Early on the morning of the 11th August 1897, Viscount Ebrington left his home at Bydown House, Swimbridge, to ride over to Simonsbath. In the evening of the same day he took up his abode in Simonsbath House for the first time, although only one room up and one down were made habitable on this occasion. Nevertheless there was some cause for celebration and on the following morning the Devon and Somerset Stag Hounds were laid on at his door.

Bydown House—a rented property—was given up on Lady Day 1898, even though there was still much work to be done on refurbishing the old house at Simonsbath, and some time was to elapse before Viscount Ebrington and his family were able to move into their new home.

It was at around this time that the demolition of John Knight's uncompleted mansion is said to have been carried out, but in fact this was not entirely true. Some parts of the mansion were certainly removed, but the remaining walls were merely lowered to more acceptable proportions and then roofed over by a firm of contractors brought in from away. No doubt the stone removed from the old building was then used in the next stage of the planned improvements, which was to extend Simonsbath House—or Lodge as it was now called—westwards as far as the old Wool Chamber.

Inside the house the dining room floor was lowered to give more height to the room. New fireplaces were built, and fine panelling, which is believed to have come from some other property owned by the Fortescue family, was fitted around one or two of the rooms, along with a splendid example of an hereditary Coat of Arms, which was placed in the entrance lounge above the fireplace. This Coat of Arms, beautifully carved, is said to be of considerable value.

Another improvement carried out at this time was to divert the main road away from the house in order to give it more privacy. New stables and a coach house were also built a short distance to the northwest. These were linked to the Lodge by a paved driveway. At the eastern end of the stable block a cottage was built for the stud groom, but as Dick Barrow spent as much of his time at Castle Hill as he did at Simonsbath, it would appear that the cottage, then known as The Stables, but for many years now as Rose Cottage, was for the most part occupied by other employees on the estate on the understanding that they provided a room and breakfast for the stud groom when he was at Simonsbath. This agreement was still in force when my good friends Harry and Margaret (Mag) Prout moved into the cottage in 1947. Mag remembers Dick Barrow as a short thickset, kind and genial man, who for over 54 years was in the service of the Fortescue family, as coachman and groom. For many of these years he was personal groom to Lady Fortescue, the wife of Viscount Ebrington, who became the 4th Lord Fortescue in 1905 on his father's death.

Dick Barrow died in 1929 and was buried at Filleigh. Among the floral tributes, one, 'To my best friend R. Barrow from Countess Fortescue', reflects the great personal loss felt by his many friends, rich and poor alike.

We do not know the exact date that Viscount Ebrington and his family took up residence at Simonsbath Lodge, but an entry in his personal diary for the 23rd July 1899, reveals that the house was by no means ready for occupation. Nevertheless it is believed that by the beginning of the hunting season in the same year—or shortly after—they had moved in, and though Viscount Ebrington was often away attending to his public duties and business affairs, their main base was at Simonsbath until after his father's death in 1905, when they moved to the family seat at Castle Hill, though still spending a part of each year at their Simonsbath Lodge.

In the year of Sir Frederic Knight's death, two cottages, which became known as Jubilee Cottages—or Villas—on account of them having been built in the year of Queen Victoria's Diamond Jubilee, were erected beside the lane leading to White Rock Cottage and the School. Local tradition has it that these cottages were intended for two of Sir Frederic Knight's employees, and that there was a race on to get them finished and in the occupation of the intended before he passed on. Maybe so, but Mrs Ivy Tucker—née Steer—tells me that it was Lord Fortescue who had promised one of these cottages to her grandfather, Richard Steer. It is possible some confusion has arisen because Richard was one of Sir Frederic's former employees before he went farming. It is not at present known who was the first occupant of the other cottage.

The Telegraph reached Simonsbath in 1898, having been extended from Exford which received it the year before. A note in G.C. Smyth-Richard's* diary dated 15.2.1898, reveals that William Kingdom had approached him to see if he could rent the old Reading Room for use as a Telegraph Office, for which he offered to pay £1 a year, and to fit it out at his own expense. Possibly William had second thoughts about his proposal on hearing that all he was to receive for each message delivered within a radius of three miles was 1d. No one I have spoken to has heard of the Reading Room being used for this purpose and it would appear that the Telegraph instruments were fitted up in the old Post Office.

* Agent to both Sir Frederic Knight and Viscount Ebrington

Jubilee Villas (South View)

*John and Bessie Hooper,
Carter and Farmer.*

*William and Emily Hunt,
Carter and Smallholder.*

West Cottages old and new, about 1910.

Westgate Cottages built 1899.

In January 1898, a builder named Southwood was instructed to proceed with the conversion of the building used to house Sir Frederic Knight's steam ploughing engine when not in use, into two cottages, but it is doubtful if much work was done there for a month or two because in February the snow was very deep on Exmoor. The steam engine was later taken down to the Tile Yard at Castle Hill, where the wheels were removed and the engine was then used as a stationary unit for some years. Its ultimate fate is not known. The ploughs and ploughing tackle were sold off.

The 'New' West Cottages were completed and occupied by April in the following year, and insured for £125 apiece. It was probably at this time that the old order of Nos 1-4 West Cottages, starting from the Challacombe end, was reversed to become Nos 1-6, as it is today, beginning from the Simonsbath end.

Living in No. 1 West Cottages at this time was George Molland who had replaced William Brian as the Estate Farm Bailiff in 1892. In 1897 he married Agnes Red, one of the daughters of William Red of Simonsbath Barton. The cottage next door was probably occupied by John Govier, a mason from North Molton, who was taken on to the estate payroll in January 1898, but by 1899 he had been replaced by Charles Balment, who remained there until about 1918. The other 'new' cottage was taken by James Welch, the estate carpenter, who when last encountered was living in the housekeeper's quarters in Simonsbath House.

In the older block of West Cottages, now numbered 4, 5 and 6 east to west, were John Hooper, William Hunt and David Hoggan, respectively. At this time all three were employed on the Exmoor Estate.

In 1899, after working for some eight years as a carter on the estate, John Hooper began farming, renting 77 acres of land, which he continued to farm from his cottage until 1920 when he was able to take the tenancy of Driver, a larger farm on the estate. He continued to prosper and by the time he retired in 1934 had done very well for himself.

William Hunt is said to have been the first outsider taken on by Viscount Ebrington after he took possession of the Exmoor and Brendon Estates. By 1901—probably before—he was living in No. 5 West Cottages, the former home of Frederick Blackmore—Sir Frederic Knight's groom. In the same year, William also began farming in a small way, but in 1908 he sold off all his stock and moved to Pinkery to take charge of the sheep herding there, returning to Simonsbath in 1912 when the herding was given up and Pinkery let as a farm.

David Hoggan, who came down from Scotland in the latter half of 1897 to work on the estate must surely have been a contender as the first outsider taken on by Viscount Ebrington. By the early part of 1898 he was living in No. 6 West Cottages, the former home of Sir Frederic Knight's gamekeeper, William Tucker, who retired in February of that year at the age of 70, and left the village shortly after.

David Hoggan, woodman and estate worker, was responsible for planting many of the trees to be seen around Simonsbath today. In the autumn of

1897 he planted thousands of spruce and hardwood trees on Cornham Knap. In January the following year he asked the Exmoor Estate Agent for a further 12,000 trees to finish the job. David also spent much of his time repairing the fences on the estate; work that he took a great pride in, and was so well done that when I became friendly with Jack Buckingham in the 1980s, he could still point to work carried out by David Hoggan and his sons three-quarters of a century before. For a short time David also rented a couple of small fields, but never progressed beyond that stage. At some time before 1906 he and his family moved to Jubilee Cottage (Villa) where he remained until 1912, when they returned to Scotland.

William Tucker's replacement as gamekeeper was John Blackmore (Frederick's son), who for some time past had been assisting the old keeper with his duties. John was employed in a similar capacity with the added responsibility of overseeing the rabbit trappers at work on the estate. John Blackmore's address in 1891 was Duredon, but by 1896 he was living in Simonsbath—we know not where. In 1908, following William Hunt's departure to Pinkery, he moved into his father's former cottage, moving on to The Stables* in or about the year 1914, remaining there until about 1929 when he returned to West Cottages, this time into No. 6, where he lived out the rest of his life. He died in October 1940. The contents of his home were sold off shortly after.

Two more cottages were built around the turn of the century, alongside the Challacombe road, just to the east of Limecombe. These cottages became known as West Gate, one of which—No. 2—had been promised to Donald MacDougal, a shepherd who came down from Scotland in 1894 to take charge of the Simonsbath Herding when Richard Steer left to take over the family smallholding. For a few years after his arrival Donald was in lodgings in and around Simonsbath, and for a short time prior to moving into his new home he was allowed an extra 2/- a week on top of his normal wages because he had nowhere to keep a cow—one of the perquisites of the job.

The other cottage at West Gate was assigned to the tenant of Simonsbath Barton for a farmworker. The first occupant of this cottage was William Webber and his family, who moved in on Lady Day 1901. William was still living in the same cottage when he died in 1935. His wife died there two years later.

A major project put in hand in Simonsbath at this time was the complete refurbishment of the saw mill and other buildings there. In a letter to Viscount Ebrington dated 18.9.1897 G. C. Smyth Richards comments that unless something was quickly done to repair the waterwheel they would be unable to use it for sawing or chaffcutting in the autumn. It is not known if temporary repairs were carried out, but in the following month plans were drawn up for a complete range of new buildings to be erected on precisely the same site.

The new buildings ranged from a sawmill and carpenter's shop to a

---

* Renamed Rose Cottage around 1915

chaff millhouse. A machine for kibbling or bruising maize was also ordered, with an initial supply of 1,000 bushels of maize. A mortar machine was also installed, which was used for grinding down limestone for use in building work. Jack Buckingham could remember this old machine and the ground lime falling into a large saucer shaped dish, from which it was then shovelled out by hand. Sadly this machine, along with a huge chaffcutter, have both been broken up for scrap.

The late Tom Little of Barnstaple could remember two men working at the sawmill in 1910, sawing out posts and making hurdles and gates, and a 'pickle pot' in which to 'dunk' them to preserve them.

Provision was also made for a generator and storage batteries. The output of the generator was 35 amps, sufficient to supply electric light to a large part of the village. Simonsbath Lodge and the stables were connected, as too was the Exmoor Forest Hotel, the Vicarage and Rose Cottage.

The waterwheel was dispensed with and replaced with a turbine. It was estimated that by taking in the waters of Ashcombe and Limecombe the turbine would produce 10 h.p., which could be doubled by taking in Bale Water. Another proposal was to take water off the River Barle, which it was estimated would give 50-60 h.p. In the end all the available sources were used. To do this a weir was constructed across the River Barle, and another across the lower reaches of Limecombe Water, just below its junction with Bale Water, where, by using a system of sluice gates, the waters from the Barle, Limecombe and Bale Water were diverted down a new leat to the mill. The old leat running along the top of the same fields was then done away with. According to Jack Buckingham the combined waters gave a maximum 40 h.p. but this was never needed.

On the higher side of the road above the saw mill—just to the west of Boevey's Restaurant—a small 30 cwt Avery cattle weighbridge was installed in 1899. It is still in its original setting although no longer in use, and must be one of the few surviving examples of its type and date.

Apart from one more cottage which we will come to shortly, there was very little further development within the village for many years, but other aspects of its history during this period are not without interest.

In August 1898 a traveller (rep.) in the employ of a Barnstaple grocer, had a narrow escape when he was caught in a terrific thunderstorm near Simonsbath. A tree abutting the road was struck by lightning just a few yards from him, continuing across the road and leaving a deep rent in the highway.*

In January of the following year a workman in the employ of Sir William Williams of Oare was returning home from Challacombe with a load of fodder when he fell off his cart near Simonsbath and a wheel of the wagon passed over his body. It was two hours before he was discovered lying unconscious in the road. He was then taken to Lord Ebrington's house at Simonsbath and Dr Jackson of North Molton was at once telegraphed for. The doctor

* *North Devon Journal* 25.8.1898

quickly made his way to the village but such was the severity of the poor man's internal injuries that he could give no hope for his recovery and he died a few hours later.*

On the 3rd February 1899, a report on a case tried at Dulverton Petty Sessions entitled 'Shocking Story from Exmoor' appeared in the *North Devon Journal*. It is not a pretty story, and fortunately such cases have been very rare in the annals of Exmoor's history.

'Henry Dear, a farm labourer, and his wife Elizabeth, were summoned by the N.S.P.C.C. for ill-treating their two children age 8 years, and 13 months respectively. The defendants occupied a three bedroom cottage near Simonsbath (not identified), the husband earning 10/- a week plus the rent free house. Inspector Minn of the N.S.P.C.C. found the house in an indescribably dirty condition without any fire, and the only food discovered was a bucket of potatoes, a little dry flour, and a drop of milk.

The woman admitted there had been no bread in the house for three days. The eldest child was covered with bruises which the mother alleged was the result of an excessive thrashing by the father. Her only clothing was a ragged frock and one undergarment, both of which were filthy. The child's face and body were so thickly covered with dirt the skin was barely visible. The infant was found lying on an old broken wood bedstead with a straw mattress and a heap of rags which were saturated and infested with vermin. It was admitted by the mother that she and her husband slept in the same bed; with the eldest child sleeping on an old 'doust' mattress in an even worse condition in the corner of the room, the only covering being an old cardigan vest and a worn out counterpane. The infant's body was badly emaciated and only weighed 14 lbs as against a normal weight of 20 lbs.

It transpired that the father—who was addicted to drink—had twice been sent to gaol for beating and neglecting the elder child. The evidence was corroborated by Lord Ebrington who paid a subsequent visit to the house with Inspector Minn, Dr Sydenham and the Master and nurse of the Dulverton Workhouse. The man was sentenced to six months' hard labour— the maximum penalty, and the woman likewise. Presumably the children were taken to the Dulverton Workhouse, which although it did not enjoy the best of reputations, must certainly have seemed like heaven to the two youngsters after the squalid conditions they had been living in; in mortal fear of their father.'

There was great sadness in the Fortescue family when, shortly after taking up residence at Simonsbath Lodge, Viscount Ebrington's second son, Geoffrey, died after a few weeks of a bronchitis related illness which developed into pneumonia. He had been very poorly on the 13th August 1900, and had had such a rotten night on the 14th that at 6am the following morning he was sent to the North Devon Infirmary at Barnstaple. At 6.45am on the 16th, Viscount Ebrington was called to his son's bedside after Geoffrey had had another rotten, restless and sleepless night and had suffered

* *North Devon Journal* 19.1.1899

a fainting fit after a severe bout of coughing. He never rallied and died at 8 o'clock the same morning. According to Viscount Ebrington's personal diary, Geoffrey never once complained during his illness, and his Lordship did not know how he was going to break the sad news to his eldest son Hugh, but Hugh was very good; the servants also. He concluded the entry in his diary with 'Pretty broken down with grief and sorrow—a bad day'. Three days later Geoffrey Faithfull Fortescue was laid to rest in Filleigh Churchyard.

In 1901, following James Fry's retirement, the William Rufus Hotel and four fields were let to a Mr R. Moyle for £105 p.a., subject to an increased rental at the end of three years if business warranted it. The hotel was then renamed Exmoor Forest Hotel and has continued so to the present day. Business does not appear to have been too brisk at this time and at the end of his three years' term Mr Moyle gave up the premises and left.

The hotel was then divided into two parts and let separately, with Thomas Wyatt taking the part nearest the main road, retaining the name of the Exmoor Forest Hotel, and the fishing rights; and George Molland—the Exmoor Estate Bailiff—taking the other part, which became known as the Temperance Hotel. George Molland's former home at No. 1 West Cottages was then made over to Charles Daniel Elworthy*, who had recently married Richard Steers' daughter Ethel.

For some years past Charlie Elworthy had been employed on the estate as a carpenter, but he was just as interested in farming and by 1910 had taken the tenancy of Honeymead Allotment; adding more land as he could afford it until by 1916 he was paying £104 a year in rent.

George Molland's tenancy of the Temperance Hotel was a short one. In September 1904, he moved into a newly completed house which had been built just below the top lane into Simonsbath Barton—adjacent to the main road to Brendon. Although the new house was officially called Barton Lane Cottage for some years, it has always been known locally as Red Brick House, on account of its construction, which was—and still is—the only house in the village built entirely of brick. With its completion, the major building and refurbishment programme within the village begun by Viscount Ebrington in 1897, came to an end, although there was of course always plenty of work for the resident carpenters and masons to do.

The next tenant of the Temperance Hotel was Thomas Elworthy—son of Thomas Bale Elworthy—who when last mentioned was farming some 57 acres of land. In 1909 Thomas had the sad misfortune to lose his' wife at the untimely age of only 36, and without her help, and left with three young children, he gave up the hotel and moved to No. 2 West Gate Cottages, the former home of Donald MacDougall, who was now running his sheep herding from the old cottage at Wheal Eliza Mine.

Although Thomas Elworthy had given up the hotel, he still retained the land he had been farming. In 1911 he married for the second time, and two years later took the tenancy of a larger farm on the estate—Warren; moving

* Son of William Elworthy—The Rev. Thompson's long time employee

on to Honeymead in 1925. He retired to Brushford near Dulverton in 1939 and died there nine years later.

Thomas Elworthy's successor at the Temperance Hotel was William Albert Steer—Richard Steer's only son—who shortly before his father's death in 1906 had taken over the adjoining Exmoor Forest Hotel when Thomas Wyatt moved to Duredon Farm. The two hotels were then again run as one unit and have been ever since.

In September 1916, on William Steer's instructions, the whole of the contents of the Exmoor Forest Hotel were auctioned off, and at the same time, the furniture from South View—one of the Jubilee Villas—was also sold. A report in the *North Devon Journal* (5.10.1916) stated that 900 lots in all were on offer which readily made good prices.

William Steer's mother, who had carried on farming at South View after his husband's death, was now living with her daughter and son-in-law, Charlie Elworthy, at West Cottages. This allowed William, his wife and daughter Ivy to move into the family home and to take over the smallholding. In 1920, William and his family moved into Cornham Farm. Two years later, at the age of 15, William's daughter Ivy became the organist at the parish church of St Lukes, a position she held for about six years.

William Steer retired from farming in 1936. He died at Exford in 1954 but was buried at Simonsbath; he was the last of his line to live and farm on Exmoor.

In 1905, William Kingdom, long time blacksmith, farmer, sub post master, parish clerk, registrar of births and deaths, school attendance officer and census enumerator, gave up the blacksmith's side of his business, but as far as is known, carried on with the rest of his interests until his death in March 1915 at the age of 76.

Ernest Kingdom—William's son—a bachelor, who for some years had been farming on his own account from the family home, took over his father's smallholding as well, and the Post Office. He gave up the latter in 1922, but carried on farming until the death of his mother in 1936. Shortly after, Ernest decided to call it a day. He had a livestock sale in September, followed by a sale of his implements, and a final clearance sale in March 1937. Among the contents on offer at his final sale was the shop counter and a writing desk. What a story that old desk could tell if only it could talk, always assuming that it belonged to William Kingdom, who in the course of carrying out his parish and other duties over a period of more than 50 years, could well have recorded half the history of Simonsbath and the parish of Exmoor upon it.

In 1938, the year after Ernest Kingdom left Simonsbath, the cottage in which he, his father and grandfather before him had lived since at least as far back as 1851, was pulled down, along with the cottage next door.

In the 1993 *Exmoor Review*, Hugh Nugent of the Malt House, North Molton, describes the discovery of a brass plate while removing a clump of pampas grass from his garden. On cleaning the plate it was found to bear the inscription 'William Kingdom, Registrar of Births and Deaths for the Exmoor District'. How the plate came to be in Mr Nugent's garden is not known, but we do know that when William Kingdom's daughter Edith, who had married her cousin—also a William Kingdom—retired from farming at Cornham in 1920, they moved into Homedale, North Molton. This house stands opposite the entrance to the Malt House and only 50 yards or so from the spot where the brass plate was found. We also know that when Ernest Kingdom left Simonsbath in 1937, that he went to live with his sister and brother-in-law at Homedale, so presumably one or the other of them brought the plate to North Molton.

One family so far unmentioned who was living in Simonsbath prior to Sir Frederic's death was that of John Charles Jones—or Christian Jones as he was known. He was not—as I had been led to believe—the son of Evan Jones, a Welsh miner who came over from South Wales in the late 1850s to work in the Exmoor iron mines, even though his son John was about the same age. John (Christian) Jones was in fact the son of Richard Jones of Barton Gate, Challacombe, and was born in 1858.

Christian Jones was certainly born with itchy feet. By 1881 he had married a Porlock girl and was living at Thorne Park, Charles, moving on to High Bray in 1884. Four children were baptised while living in the parish, two on the same day in 1884 and two similarly in 1889, though neither pair were twins. William John, one of the first pair baptised, was also buried there in 1893. Shortly after, Christian Jones and his family moved to Winstitchen on the Exmoor Estate, working as a labourer there. Two more children were baptised in 1894, in Simonsbath Church, and at some time shortly before Sir Frederic Knight's death Christian Jones is said to have become the caretaker of Simonsbath House, where presumably he and his family lived in the caretaker's quarters, moving on to Driver Cot when Viscount Ebrington took over the Exmoor Estate in 1897. In the same year another child was baptised at Simonsbath but by 1904 Christian Jones and his family had moved to White Rock Cottage, and it was there that he got a foot on the farming ladder in the usual way on Exmoor, by renting a couple of cows and a little land on which to put them. By 1909 he was living and farming in the same manner at Limecombe, moving on to No. 5 West Cottages in or about the year 1916, where he rented the cottage and two fields for £13 a year. In the early part of 1918 Christian Jones was able to take the tenancy of the Cloven Rocks smallholding at a rental of £38 a year, moving on to Winstitchen Farm in 1922, where he remained until his retirement in 1931. He died five years later in the cottage adjoining Kipscombe Farmhouse, Countisbury; the farm there being occupied by his daughter Alice and her husband Will Hobbs. Will, too, was a former employee on the Exmoor Estate, having been shepherd-in-charge of the Hoar Oak Herding from 1913-1932.

Christian Jones is remembered by his granddaughter Dorothy Little—née Jones—late of Simonsbath but now living in North Molton, as a quiet man, who when he was farming, strongly objected to anyone who attempted to use dogs to drive his cows. His sons Richard (Dick), Sidney (Sid) and John (Jack) who was also known as Johnny Socks, to distinguish him from his cousin John H. Jones (Postie Jones)—who we will come to in a moment—all worked for Lord Fortescue.

Dick Jones, who married in 1906, took over White Rock Cottage when his parents moved to Limecombe, and shortly after, began farming in the traditional Exmoor manner. He moved on to Jubilee Villa, which at this time was—like the cottage next door—known as South View. When his father moved to Winstitchen Farm in 1922, Dick took over his former smallholding at Cloven Rocks, moving on, in or about the year 1929, to Red Deer Farm on the Simonsbath-Exford road. Sadly, just as Dick and his wife Sarah were beginning to prosper by taking in visitors and doing cream teas in conjunction with their farming activities, Sarah died (1936), and though Dick and his youngest daughter Hilda carried on for a little longer, she was too young to cope with all the work and responsibility and Dick decided to call it a day.

For a time after he gave up farming Dick Jones did a bit of jobbing labouring around Simonsbath. He then moved down to the Barnstaple area, but returned to Simonsbath in 1939 to live with his daughter Hilda and her husband George Clatworthy who were now living at West Gate. In 1947, Cloven Rocks was without a tenant, so Dick took it, and along with his daughter and son-in-law moved in and began farming again, remaining there until he retired in 1953. Dick spent the rest of his life living with one or other of his three daughters. He died at Little Crocombe, Simonsbath, the home of his daughter Dorothy and son-in-law Will Little in 1971 at the age of 84.

Sid Jones was for 17 years a shepherd on the Exmoor Estate, before moving on to Riscombe, Exford, where he worked for the Bowater family for some years. Jack Jones (Johnny Socks) was also a shepherd on the estate for many years, but at the time he lived at Rose Cottage (1929-1932) was a general labourer. In the latter year, Jack moved to Badgworthy to take the sheep-herding there, which Lord Fortescue had leased back in 1926, remaining there until 1940 when the army commandeered Badgworthy as part of their training area. Jack then moved to Blackpits. He gave up his herding in 1946, sold his surplus furniture and effects, along with seven ferrets and three well trained sheep dogs, and moved to Coventry to be near his daughter Winifred. At the time of writing (March 1993) he is still living there and will be 96 this year.

Another so far unmentioned inhabitant of Simonsbath in Sir Frederic Knight's time was William Grant, a farmworker from Challacombe who took up residence in the cottage adjoining the old Post Office in 1891. By 1904 he had moved on to Bale Water and was renting the cottage there and a few acres of land for which he was paying £23.10.0 a year.

William Grant's successor in the cottage next to the old Post Office was John H. Jones, or Postie Jones as he was known. He was a nephew of Christian Jones. For some years prior to the First World War he was employed by Lord Fortescue as a gardener at the Lodge, before taking on the post round, delivering mail by horseback in the Simonsbath area, a job he continued to do for many years.

Postie Jones had a lodger, Bill Staddon, who also worked on the estate. In the course of his duties one morning he made a rather startling discovery. The story was recorded in the *North Devon Journal* (28.4.1910) under the heading 'An Exmoor Sensation', which described the tragic death of a young woman visitor to Simonsbath, the gist of which is as follows:

'On Monday last week, on a lonely spot near Simonsbath Mr William Staddon, in the employ of Lord Fortescue, discovered a young lady lying in an unconscious state in a niche in a hayrick. Staddon was pulling out some hay with a fork when he made his startling discovery. Near the lady was a handbag which contained tablets of a poisonous nature and some poison in a bottle. The stranger was immediately conveyed to the residence of the Rev. Ramsay—Vicar of Exmoor—and a doctor wired for. He quickly arrived but despite all that medical skill could devise the lady never regained consciousness and passed away on Wednesday.

The deceased, whose name was Harriet Mabel Willand, aged about 30, had been staying at Market Lavington, Wiltshire, with friends. She left them on the 15th, saying she was going flower gathering, but did not return. She travelled to Exeter on the night mail train, reaching St Davids Station about 3am. She then went to the Great Western Hotel, and while there was seen by a servant to destroy several letters and to tear the corner off a handkerchief, which presumably bore her name.

At 7.15am on the same morning, Harriet Willand left Exeter on the train bound for Dulverton Station, and on arrival at that station made inquiries as to where she could get a conveyance to drive her to Simonsbath, a distance of 14 miles from Dulverton. This was arranged by Mr C. W. Neider, the proprietor of the Carnarvon Hotel, and on the way she commented to the driver about the beautiful scenery. She also asked him if Simonsbath was a more secluded spot than Dartmoor.

On arrival at the village she alighted at the Exmoor Forest Hotel where she had tea and afterwards went for a walk. She was not seen again until she was found by William Staddon on Monday morning.

At the inquest on Friday the jury returned a verdict that the deceased had died from heart failure through taking poisonous sulphur tablets. Preparations were then made for burying her in the Simonsbath churchyard and an order given for a parish coffin. This however was stopped when relations appeared on the scene, and the deceased was then conveyed to Dulverton and then by rail to London, for burial there.'

According to Margaret (Mag) Prout of Rose Cottage, the young lady was found in a shed that was for many years used for storing hay. It was situated in the second field on the east side of the Brendon road, above the top entrance into Simonsbath Barton.[1]

Bill Staddon was one of two horsemen employed on the estate farm at this time. The other was George Webber, the son of William of No. 1 West Gate Cottages. The horsemen each had a pair of carthorses to look after. They were kept in stables at the top end of what is now the car park to Boeveys Restaurant. George Webber's stable was on the left; Bill Staddon's on the right. The upper level of these stables was for many years used as a bothy for Lord Fortescue's under-grooms when the family was in residence at the Lodge, the head groom residing at Rose Cottage.

Besides the normal horsework on the estate farm, the two horsemen were also responsible for delivering groceries to the outlying farms in hand and the shepherds' cottages, a month's supply at a time. Orders for groceries were sent by post to Jack Crang, grocer of North Molton, who delivered them as far as Simonsbath. They were then taken on by horse and cart. When Mag—daughter of Jack Little—was living with her parents at Badgworthy (1908-1916) her mother also used to have a sack of barley meal; a sack of maize meal for pigs and poultry, and a sack of flour for making bread etc., each month from Mr Gammon, miller of Heasley Mill. They were delivered by the same arrangement.

There was so much going on in and around the village of Simonsbath in the closing years of the 19th C. and first two decades of the 20th C., that it is all but impossible to keep track of events, or for that matter the movement of people into and out of the village.

When Lord Fortescue took possession of the Exmoor Estate in 1897, he found he had just six tenants within the village, renting a total of 960 acres of land and paying a combined rental of £691. Of this land 620 acres went with Simonsbath Barton, leaving 340 acres split between the five smallholders. By 1909, after William Red had reduced the land he was renting at the Barton to 244 acres, the number of smallholders in the village rose to 13, renting 556 acres in all, for which they were paying Lord Fortescue rents amounting to £565. At this time many of the tenants still worked either full or part time on the estate—their sons also. A further 10 cottages in the village were occupied rent free by other estate employees.

The policy of letting a little land to the ordinary working men, begun by Frederic Knight in the late 1850s and much encouraged by Lord Fortescue when he took over the Exmoor Estate is—I believe—unique in the annals of English history. Personally I have not come across a similar example in this country in this period of time, or for that matter any other, where the common working man was given such an opportunity to better himself, and some of these men who progressed to larger farms, ended up with quite considerable fortunes.

When William Kingdom gave up the blacksmith's side of his business in 1905, William Lavercombe, a blacksmith from Bratton Fleming took over. He moved into No. 6 West Cottages, renting the cottage, garden and smithy for £9.10.0. a year: a rent that was increased later when he too began to farm a few acres of land.

According to the Church Vestry Minutes Book, William Lavercombe took over the duties of Parish Clerk following William Kingdom's death in 1915. He also undertook the job of keeping the church and churchyard paths clean and tidy, and to cut the grass in the churchyard twice a year, duties that for many years before his death had been carried out by John Steer of White Rock. The remuneration paid at this time was £8.13.6. p.a., in addition to

*George Webber (Horseman) outside Viscount Ebrington's stables,
with Rose Cottage on the Right.*

*Robert Tait Little and George Molland, Head Shepherd and Bailiff
respectively to both Frederic Knight and Viscount Ebrington.*

St. Lukes Church Choir 1906.

Miss Richards?, Rev. Ramsay, William Kingdom (Blacksmith)
(2nd Row) Hetty Kingdom, Harry Watts, Mrs Ramsay, Polly Richards,
(3rd Row) Ernest Kingdom, Charlie Elworthy, Wavey Coward,
Mary Elworthy, N.K., Mrs. Gammin
(Front Row) David Hoggan's children.

William Lavercombe, Blacksmith, Smallholder and Postman.

any fees payable by custom to Parish Clerk and Sexton. In 1917, William Lavercombe had his annual salary increased to £10, but early in the following year when he gave up the smithy and moved to Bale Water to become a full time farmer, he also gave up his part time job, though still offering his services as Sexton as far as he was able. For some years William also did one of the three local post rounds, which his daughter Frances took over when he retired.

Margaret Lavercombe—William's wife—died in 1929. Four years later he retired from farming and gave up Bale Water, moving into the village to White Rock where he kept a few hens and pottered about. In 1941 he sold his poultry and appliances and moved to Winsford, where he died in 1954 at the age of 84. He too is buried at Simonsbath. For a few years from 1923-1930, he was Church Warden of the Exmoor Parish Church.

By 1912, James Welch—estate carpenter for many years—had moved on and Harry Watts, who for a time also worked on the estate, was living in his former home. This was shortly after Harry's marriage to Lily Crang of North Molton. Their daughter, Mrs Anne Buckingham—now and for many years past a resident of North Molton—tells me that when her parents were living at No. 3 West Cottages her mother ran a little shop there, while her father rented a few acres of land and began farming.

Harry Watts and his wife and daughter moved off the Exmoor Estate in 1916 to Kinsford, but continued to rent land from Lord Fortescue and by 1920 Harry was able to take the tenancy of Horsen Farm, which he continued to farm until 1942 when he semi-retired to Simonsbath.

The next occupant of No. 3 West Cottages was Jack Little—Mag's father—shepherd of Badgworthy, who, partly as a result of the sale of the Brendon Estate—which included Badgworthy—by Lord Fortescue to Sir Edward Mortimer Mountain in 1916, and partly because of the need to be nearer a school for his children's education, moved to Simonsbath. Despite the rough journey from Badgworthy over Brendon Common to the main road to Simonsbath, not one item of crockery was broken, nor one piece of furniture damaged during the transportation by horse and cart, so Mag informs me.

Jack was the eldest son of William Little, one of Frederic Knight's original Scottish shepherds. From an early age he had wanted a herding of his own, but as there were no vacancies for a shepherd when he became old enough, he went down to Filleigh to learn the trade of a mason on the Castle Hill Estate. He helped Walter Jennings—the Exmoor Estate mason—build the fine tomb in Simonsbath Churchyard, where Sir Frederic Knight, his wife and only son are buried and also had a hand in building Stables Cottage (Rose Cottage) where his daughter Mag has lived for the past 46 years.

At the first opportunity—1903—Jack was able to return to his first love, and took the Pinkery Herding, moving on to Badgworthy in 1908. After this herding was given up, a new herding, known as Blackpits, was created, which Jack ran from West Cottages until 1921, when he and his family were at last able to move into a newly constructed 'tin' bungalow at Blackpits which should have been built in 1916, but was postponed because of the First World War.

Memories of Simonsbath during the First World War are hazy now, but there appears to have been no great hardship within the village. The war was far away, with communications of its progress limited to word of mouth, the telegraph, occcasional letters home and one newspaper a week around which everybody crowded to get the latest news. There was as yet no commercial radio.

Towards the end of the war G. C. Smyth Richards drove over to Simonsbath to see about coal rationing, but as all of the villagers had unlimited supplies of peat from their own turf pits for their Bodley stoves and open fires, the rationing of coal gave little cause for concern.

A few of the Simonsbath men went off to war. Sid Jones and his brother Jack joined the Navy, George Webber, Henry and Walter Hunt—the Army. Towards the end of the war, Walter Hunt, who had seen action in Gallipoli, Egypt and Palestine, and had risen to the rank of Sergeant, was sent to the Western Front with his unit—the 16th Battalion, Devon Dismounted Hussars Territorial Force. During a night reconnaisance patrol with three men in October 1918 they met a German patrol of 15 men. Walter and his party charged them, killing the officer in charge, wounding others, and escorted the whole back to his headquarters; an action for which he was awarded the D.C.M.

All of the Simonsbath men who had gone off to war returned safely, Walter and Henry Hunt to their parents William and Emily Hunt, who—since Pinkery had been let as a farm—had been living at No. 2 West Gate, having taken over the cottage and land formerly rented by Thomas Elworthy, who had now moved on to Warren Farm.

William Hunt was by trade a tailor, and by all accounts a very good one, but he had chosen to embark on a career as a carter on the Exmoor Estate, before becoming a farmer, which, following his brief stint as a shepherd he had now returned to.

William and his sons were good judges where horses were concerned and made money from their dealings. By the early 1920s both sons were married and farming on their own account. They also worked as contractors on the district roads, hauling material for repairs and road widening schemes.

Walter Hunt's wife died in 1927, leaving him with two small children, who for a few years after their mother's death were cared for by relatives at Chittlehampton, while Walter returned home to live with his parents. No. 4 West Cottages, where he had been living, was then taken over by his brother Henry.

In 1933, following William Lavercombe's departure from Bale Water, William Hunt took over the tenancy of the farm: Walter moving there with them. In the same year he married again. It would appear that when the Hunts moved to Bale Water, Walter had kept on the cottage and land at West Gate, because in the following year, according to the *North Devon Journal* (30.8.1934) he had a live and dead stock sale there, along with his furniture, on account that he was leaving. He is known to have moved about a bit after this, and that from 1937-1940 he was living in a converted railway carriage at Moles Chamber, looking after stock for the May brothers on the Acland Allotment and continued to do so after moving into the stockman's cottage at Aclands.

William Hunt gave up Bale Water in 1939, whereupon it became the kennels for the Exmoor Foxhounds, and has been ever since. William returned to West Gate; not into his former home, but into the cottage next door. He remained there until his death in 1955 at the age of 83.

Walter Hunt also returned to Simonsbath and for a few years lived next door to his parents. He sold up in 1957 and moved to Bratton Fleming. His brother Henry moved out of the village at some time around 1937. He lived at Honeymead for many years, working on the roads for the District Council.

In some ways 1916 was quite an eventful year as far as the inhabitants of Simonsbath were concerned. It had begun with exceptionally heavy falls of snow; comparable with the severe blizzards of January 1861; March 1878; January 1881 and February 1898, to name but a few of the worst.

On 4th March G. C. Smyth Richards recorded in his diary that there were 26 men and 3 horses clearing the blocked road from South Molton to Simonsbath, but no sooner was it cleared for traffic than it was blocked again by a further fall of snow.

Once again work was begun to clear a passage through, as by this time the sheep on Exmoor were suffering from want of feed, and it was imperative the road was opened as quickly as possible. The snow was cleared, and for a day or two the road remained open, allowing some fodder to be brought in, but on 28th March a further fall of snow blocked it again and it was not until early April that a thaw set in and it was possible to pass freely into and out of Simonsbath once more.

When Mag started school at Simonsbath in September 1916 at the age of seven, there were 41 pupils in attendance, double the number there when the late Tom Little of Barnstaple was a pupil in 1910. Mrs Lena White was the current school mistress, having taken over from Mrs Nichols in 1898 and because of the rise in pupil numbers there was also an assistant teacher, Miss Wilminshurst.

Shortly after Mag became a pupil at the village school, she joined the Sunday School at the parish church, and a little later became a member of the church choir. A very good choir it was in those days with some exceptionally fine voices. The choir had been much encouraged by the Rev. Ramsay when he was Vicar of Exmoor from 1904-1916. It was his custom to treat the members of the choir to an annual supper and an evening of entertainment. At one such treat—recorded in the *North Devon Journal* (19.1.1911)—22 guests at down to an excellent supper at the Vicarage and afterwards adjourned to the schoolroom where 40 more of their friends were assembled for an evening of dancing and song. 'Three Blind Mice' was sung by three of the village children, the Misses Janie Molland—George Molland's daughter—her cousin Edith Richards and Annie Beer—Mrs William Steer's niece. Their rendering of the nursery rhyme nearly brought the house down. Others who contributed songs and duets were Mrs John (Jack) Elworthy, Mrs John Kingdom and Miss Kingdom, Mr Ernest Kingdom and Mr Harry Watts. Refreshments were handed around at 10pm, after which dancing was resumed with renewed vigour until 11pm, when they all made their way home after a most enjoyable evening.

On one occasion in church, Mag can remember William Lavercombe—a choir member—holding up a sixpence to Charlie Elworthy—another member—as a bet as to who could sing the loudest, but does not now recall who won the bet.

It was in 1916 too, that Jack Elworthy, who had been renting his father's former holding at Lower House since 1910, took the tenancy of the Exmoor Forest Hotel, whilst still retaining the lands and cottage he had been renting, along with the cottage next door, which his father appears to have taken over when Richard Steer moved to South View, thus doubling the accommodation at Lower House, where, because of large families and a shortage of space when it was two cottages, some of the children slept in the roof area of the single storey buildings, but they did have some light as windows had been let into the end walls. There was a similar arrangement at White Rock Cottage.

In 1918, Jack Elworthy's wife Mary asked G. C. Smyth Richards if she could have the tenancy of the hotel in her name, Jack to guarantee the rent. Shortly after, Mary's brother William Watts, who had just returned from the war, moved from North Molton with his wife and family into Lower House, Simonsbath, which had been retained when Jack and Mary moved into the hotel.

Olive Vigars of Bossington, William Watts' daughter, has kindly allowed me to have a look at a notebook written by her father shortly before he died in 1983 at the age of 93. These notes, written in a beautiful copperplate hand, detail important moments and incidents in his long life, and from them I have picked out those parts relevant to the history of Simonsbath.

Mary Elworthy brought her first car, an Overland, from Moors Garage, South Molton in 1919, at a cost of £525, for use as a taxi at the hotel, and her brother William, after instructions on how to drive it and carry out day-to-day maintenance, took on the job of taxi driver, taking out his driving licence on 25th October 1919. He held a clean licence for 58 years before deciding to call it a day. The licence for the car in 1919 was £12 a year.

Business at the hotel in the 1920s was brisk, so much so that in 1921 Mary bought a second Overland, which was driven by her cousin Seymour Watts, who took over Postie Jones' cottage next door to the Old Post Office, when Postie and his family, along with their lodger Bill Staddon moved to West Cottages following Jack Little's departure to Blackpits. In winter time when there was little demand for a taxi service, William and Seymour carried out maintenance work in the hotel and helped out on the farm.

At about the time Mary Elworthy purchased her second car she is thought to have had two petrol pumps installed. They were not on the site of a later petrol pump above the hotel, but on the opposite side of the road below

Overland open tourer, Driver William Watts at Brendon Two Gates 1921.

Austin 12 open tourer outside Exmoor Forest Hotel 1925.
Driver William Watts.

Austin 20 saloon on Brendon Common with Miss Dickens 1930.
Driver William Watts.

Mary Elworthy's Petrol pumps. Group, Jack Watts, mounted, William and Mabel Watts, (Front row) Ada Mary Watts (Seymours daughter) and Renee and Olive Watts.

Exmoor Forest Hotel.

the line of the hotel, at a point opposite the higher end of the Pound Cottage row.

During the early 1920s William and Seymour Watts were kept busy collecting visitors from the station and taking them joyriding around the countryside, though in view of the bad state of the roads in those days, with no tarmac, perhaps joyriding is not the right description. William was out driving one day when he found himself in the same ruts as a car coming towards him, so he backed back for some distance until he could get out of the ruts to enable the other car to pass. Money was plentiful. One day William picked up £7.12.6. in tips, at a time when his wages were £1.12.0. a week, plus a rent- and rate-free cottage and plenty of milk.

By 1930, most visitors to Simonsbath had their own cars and there was less demand for a taxi service, so Mary bought a two ton lorry as there was a new road being built nearby for the Somerst County Council, and plenty of work for it.

Both of the Overland cars had been replaced with Austins by 1925 and when new cars were needed it was Austins again. Seymour Watts moved on in the early 1930s; his place was taken by Charlie Holloway from North Molton, who lived in at the hotel.

Mary Elworthy's cars were not the first in Simonsbath. That honour belongs to George Molland, the Exmoor Estate Bailiff, who was supplied with a Trojan in 1917. By all accounts George was not the best of drivers. He tended to forget he was driving a car and talked to it as he did his horse, expecting it to obey his every command. He was very generous in offering lifts, but the movelty of riding in a motor car appears to have very quickly worn off, and few were brave enough to accept another such offer.

George Molland was a little forgetful in other ways. On one occasion on returning from South Molton he said to Bill Staddon 'I fancy I've forgotten something Will but can't think what it is'. Will replied, 'All I can tell you Maister is that when you left home this morning you had Mrs Molland with you'. 'Dang me' said George 'I knew I'd forgotten something'.

The story of the reopening of the Exmoor iron mines in 1908 was fully described in *The Heritage of Exmoor*. There is little to add except that Henry Roberts, the mine manager, lived for a short time in one of the West Cottages, and for about three years at Jubilee Villa, and that Will Welch, a son of James Welch—estate carpenter for many years—sawed out the timber used in the mines and for casing the shafts.   .

Will Welch, also a carpenter on the estate, divided his time between working in the sawmill and repairs to estate property. After his father left Simonsbath, Will lodged with Jack and Mary Elworthy at the hotel and later with Eric and Gwen Watts at Duredon. While lodging with the latter it was his custom to go to Rose Cottage every working day for a cup of tea to go with his packed lunch. According to Mag he never had much to say but used to read her newspaper and then fall asleep, awakening—without fail—at exactly three minutes before it was time to return to the sawmill.

Will Welch was a tall thin man who only smoked on Sundays. He never married although he did for a time do a bit of courting. All went well until he found his lady friend with another man. That was the end of all romance for Will.

In the early months of 1918 some of the Spruce and Larch plantations in the vicinity of the village, which had been laid down by Sir Frederic Knight many years before, and which had greatly enhanced the charm and beauty of the Simonsbath scene, were sold to the Government Timber Buying Agency—the trees having now reached maturity. Because of the war and a shortage of labour the timber fellers were a pretty motley crew, including a gang of Portuguese, for whom a wooden hut was erected in front of the back door of South View, for sleeping quarters. The beds were made of wire netting, stretched over wooden frames.

The Portuguese were gone from Simonsbath when William—Taffy—Grant arrived in Simonsbath shortly after the war had ended. The remaining timber fellers were a mixed bunch from a wide area. Taffy had been born at Limecombe, but left Exmoor with his parents when he was only a few months old, bound for South Wales where his father had obtained work in the coal mines. Taffy followed him down the pit as soon as he was old enough. As soon as war broke out he joined the Navy, and having no desire to return to the coal mines when war ended, he wrote to his uncles at Bale Water and Cloven Rocks to see if they had anything to offer, but as they were both on the point of giving up their smallholdings they could not help him. There was, however, a vacancy working a portable sawmill on the estate, in conjunction with the timber fellers. Taffy got the job but couldn't stand the noise and on hearing that it was proposed to build a light railway from Simonsbath to Flexbarrow—about a mile or so below the village—to bring out the timber there, he volunteered his services, and along with Postie Jones laid down the line. On completion, Taffy got the job of engine driver of a little petrol driven engine which hauled two flat bottomed timber wagons capable of carrying 20ft lengths of timber.

Some of the village children—my good friend Mag among them—used to ride down to Flexbarrow on the empty wagons, walking up behind them when loaded. This unique railway, the only mechanically powered one ever built on Exmoor Proper, was taken up when the timber felling operations were competed, and sold to the proprietors of a brick yard in the Birmingham area.

By the time Postie Jones moved to West Cottages in 1921, he was renting a couple of fields, and over the next few years he was able to add a few more. Postie's wife died in 1927. He remarried the following year and it is a well known fact that it was his second wife, Mary, who did most of the work on the farm; Postie taking himself off to the pub as soon as he had finished his round.

It does seem a little odd to me that although the typical village cottage of yesteryear had a large garden attached in which to grow a succession of vegetables to provide for the typically large families of those times, that this was not the case at Simonsbath, where even today there are few cottages with more than a tiny patch of grass and the odd flower bed. Why this should be so is not easy to determine, but it is not thought that the height of the village above sea level, or the climate, had any bearing on the matter, so it probably has more to do with John Knight's early policy of using such cottages as were built to house gangs of labourers on the bothy system; not married men and their families. With this type of workforce there would have been little need for gardens.

Be that as it may, John Knight was certainly aware of the benefits to be had from a good garden and as early as 1836 James Jewell was busy walling around a new garden, just to the north of Simonsbath House and the shelter belt of trees, which was not—it is believed—the site of the original garden to the house. According to local tradition this was situated adjacent to, and east of the Brendon road, just above the line of the top lane into the Barton and the newer road into the estate farm buildings.

As far as Simonsbath House is concerned, John Knight's 'new garden' appears to have gone out of use a long time ago, but parts of it have—since the early years of this century—been tilled by the inhabitants of cottages within the village, including Rose Cottage, White Rock Cottage and the Schoolhouse, Jubilee Villa and South View, also the cottage adjoining the old Post Office, and more recently No. 2 West Cottages and Diana Lodge.

The vegetable garden belonging to Lower House was situated between the lane at the bottom of Birch Cleave Wood and the lane leading into the river meadow—immediately to the east end of the farm buildings. In the second decade of this century there was also a garden in the adjoining meadow a little further down Birch Cleave Lane. This plot was adjacent to a small building in the corner of the field, but no trace of either is now to be found, nor is it known who tilled it, unless it was Joseph Steer and his sons.

Another garden, in this case closer to home, was that of the Exmoor Forest Hotel, which lay adjacent to Ashcombe Water, above the building now used as a tearoom.

The vegetable garden of the old Post Office was situated in the south eastern corner of the field abutting on to the lower lane into the Barton and the road to Challacombe, which was a logical place to have it seeing as how William Kingdom—and later his son Ernest—rented the field in which it stood. The same can be said of Lower House, and the garden in the adjoining field, but this practice does not appear to have been followed by the tenants of other smallholdings within the village.

The gardens that went with West Cottages, apart from No. 1 which has always adjoined the house, were in the field above the Challacombe road, between the cottages and Ernest Kingdom's garden. No. 2 West Gate Cottage also had a garden in this piece of ground, but at one time also had a small plot below the road, opposite the cottage. The garden of the adjoining cottage was—and still is—on the bank above the cottage.

There was one other garden near West Cottages. This adjoined the field boundary hedge above. It is believed that this plot was for some years tilled by a workman living in part of the Barton farmhouse, but like the gardens of the cottages below, and those of No. 2 West Gate Cottages and the old Post Office, was returned to the field from which it was taken, in 1970.

When Mag was at school at Simonsbath, each pupil had his or her own little garden plot within the school grounds, each measuring 8ft by 5ft. The girls sowed packets of flower seeds in their plots; the boys grew vegetables in theirs, and great pleasure was had from obtaining a good show of flowers or a rich harvest of vegetables. At a later date, when Miss Olive Badger was head mistress of the school, she asked Lord Fortescue if she could have more ground for her pupils, and he let her have the land where the original garden of Simonsbath House is said to have been.

By the early 1920s there had been further changes of occupants of cottages within the village. Tom Little* shepherd of the Limecombe Herding from 1892-1919, had now given up his herding and was living at White Rock with his wife Edie—daughter of Christian Jones—and son Bob. Three years later we find them at South View and farming, but in Tommy's case there was no need to start off in the traditional Exmoor manner with a couple of rented cows and the land on which to keep them, because under the terms of his father's will, and with his own savings, he had accumulated the princely sum of £1,000. It is doubtful if any farmer who came from the ordinary working classes on Exmoor ever had a better start, and with this kind of money behind him Tommy should have gone far, and later, when he moved on to Cloven Rocks, success seemed assured. Unfortunately there was little profit to be had from farming in the 1930s and Tommy later returned to White Rock. It is believed that when he retired from farming it was with less money than he started out with. Farming, then as now, needs more than an element of luck to be successful.

Tommy Little, nicknamed I, I, because of a slight stutter, was a bit of a character. In a very open sort of way he would 'borrow' things belonging to his fellow villagers. If it was a tool, as was often the case, he would, on being accused of taking it, set off for his shed, take out the item in question and hand it back without a protest. Anything 'borrowed' by Tommy was always well looked after and where appropriate, well oiled.

On one occasion Tommy 'borrowed' the wire rabbit netting from around a neighbour's garden and put it up around his own only a short distance away. It was so blatantly obvious what he had been up to it was unbelievable to think he could get away with it, but this did not seem to worry Tommy.

Tommy Little was still living at White Rock in the mid-1950s, but shortly after, he and his wife moved to Timberscombe to live with their son. At the time of his death there was a blizzard raging on Exmoor, so Tommy was buried at Timberscombe, not Simonsbath as had been intended.

When William Lavercombe the village blacksmith moved to Bale Water in 1918, the Smithy and his former home were taken over by Carl Cook Rich, or Charlie Rich as he was known; a blacksmith from Williton.

In 1920, with an increasing number of motor vehicles passing through the

* Uncle of the late Tom Little of Barnstaple

village, Charlie Rich approached G. C. Smyth Richards to see if he could have a petrol supply. It is not known if a petrol supply was granted at this time; the first delivery of petrol of which we have record in the Fortescue Estate Account Books, was made in May 1928, when 80 gallons were delivered in two gallon tins at a cost of 1s.6d. a gallon. A similar quantity was delivered in the following month. The first bulk delivery, also 80 gallons, was in August the same year, at a slightly reduced price. The next delivery was 200 gallons in September, which cost £14.7.6. Charlie also became an agent for T. H. Moor, Ironmonger of South Molton, supplying among other items oil lamps and the paraffin to fuel them. He was also a stockist of animal feeding stuffs.

In 1928, Mary Rich—Charlie's wife—died at the age of 36, leaving him with a young family to raise. With a business to run and a living to make it was a difficult time for him so some of his children were taken to Williton to live with relatives. Shortly after, Charlie married again and had three more children by his second wife, Amy. At the time of his second marriage he was living at South View, having taken over the White Rock smallholding; Tommy Little having moved on to Cloven Rocks.

Although Charlie Rich continued to provide such blacksmith's services as were required, assisted by another blacksmith, Joe Davis, who was living in, much of his income was now derived from his farming activities, and by the time of his death at the age of 51 in 1944 he had built up a useful herd of 21 cattle and 280 sheep and lambs, which were advertised for sale in the *North Devon Journal* (13.4.1944) along with his blacksmith's tools, and sold off shortly after.

Amy Rich and her family then moved back to West Cottages, along with their lodger, Joe Davis, who continued to run the smithy for a year or two. He was the last resident blacksmith in Simonsbath.

For some years after her husband's death, Amy Rich continued on as caretaker at the village school; duties she had formerly shared with her husband. Amy and her family left the village in 1955 and moved to Leeds to be near her married daughter. She is still living there.

Charlie Balment, estate mason since 1899, left Simonsbath in 1919. His cottage was taken by Frank Vigars, who before Lord Fortescue sold his Lamerton Estate near Tavistock in 1897, had worked as a mason there. Frank's father was the Lamerton Estate Bailiff. There is some evidence to suggest that Frank came to Exmoor shortly after the Lamerton Estate was sold, to work on the Exmoor Estate.

According to Frank Vigar's son—also Frank—late of Simonsbath and Honeymead but now living in Bossington near Porlock, his father, then a single man, lodged for a time at Toms Hill and also in Simonsbath. He was probably living in the village when he sent a postcard of the Simonsbath Choir—see opposite—to his aunt who was living in Lewisham. The postmark was dated January 19th 1907.

Frank Vigars senior married Minnie Buckingham, the daughter of John Buckingham of Picked Stones in 1912. For about seven years or so after their marriage they lived at Porlock, before moving into No. 2 West Cottages. Three years later, in 1922, they moved to Jubilee Villa, where they opened a new Post Office; the old one run by William Kingdom and his son Ernest for more than 40 years having now closed.

Minnie Vigars ran an excellent shop at the Post Office for many years, while Frank combined his duties as Sub-Postmaster with his trade as a mason on the estate. They retired in 1953 and went to Goodleigh to live. Frank died in 1965, Minnie in 1970.

There were two George Webbers living in Simonsbath in the 1920s; one—Horseman George—has already been mentioned. For a short time after his marriage in 1920 he lived in No. 5 West Cottages, moving into No. 2 when Frank Vigars moved to Jubilee Villa. George, a staunch churchman, and one of the few who supported the Rev. Surtees during his troubled term of office, was Church Warden from 1935-1945, and with his wife were caretakers of the church for many years. By the time World War II began they were living in Rose Cottage, having taken it over from Tony Leworthy who for a few years from 1932-1939, worked on the estate. In 1945, ill health forced George Webber into an early retirement and they left the village to live near his wife's relatives at Devizes. Later they returned to the Exmoor area, and at the time of George's death in 1959 were living at Lower North Radworthy, Heasley Mill. Frances Emily Webber died at Beech House, South Molton in 1982 at the age of 91.

The other George Webber employed on the estate was a carpenter, who with his wife were also caretakers at Simonsbath Lodge. When the Fortescue family were in residence there George and his wife lived at White Rock. At other times they lived in the caretaker's quarters in the old house. In 1945, the Webbers sold up the contents of what was then known as Lodge Cottage and gave up their cottage at White Rock, and moved down to Filleigh, where George continued to work as a carpenter for Lord Fortescue on the Castle Hill Estate.

Another newcomer to the village in the early 1920s was Eli Jones, who was known as Withypool Jones on account of this being the place of his birth, and to distinguish him from Christian and Postie Jones and members of their families, to whom Eli was not related. During the course of his life, Eli married three times, his second and third wives being sisters of his first.

By 1925 Eli Jones was on the Exmoor Estate Rent Roll and farming land to the value of £47.1.6. p.a. He lived at No. 5 West Cottages, remaining there until he retired to North Molton in 1939, where he died two years later.

A Club known as the Exmoor Rifle Club was formed in Simonsbath in 1905, with an outdoor range in the quarry adjoining the buildings opposite the Exmoor Forest Hotel, now being converted into a dwelling house by David Little, and an indoor range in the old cart shed—now Boevey's Restaurant—which was illuminated by electric light supplied by the power plant at the sawmill.

There were certainly some first class shots on Exmoor, and in a keenly contested shooting match, recorded in the *North Devon Journal* (15.2.1923) the star prize, a silver mounted biscuit barrel presented by Mrs Bessie Hooper of Driver Farm was won by Bill Welch with a score of 299 out of a possible 300. He was closely folowed by Charlie Elworthy with 296, and Postie Jones with 295.

There was little to choose between Bill Welch and Charlie Elworthy where shooting was concerned, one or the other usually being the winner. Charlie was still competing in club events many years later when his eyesight was badly affected by cataracts. Every year he would say it was time to make way for the youngsters, but it was a long time before any of them were able to outshoot him.

Charlie Elworthy died in 1950 at the age of 75. The contents of his cottage were sold off shortly after. They included a single barrel shotgun and his beloved .22 rifle. Also sold at this time was some of the fine furniture he had made for himself over the years, including a kneehole rolltop desk, two grandfather clocks and a violin. My good friend Mag remembers one grandfather clock made by Charlie Elworthy, which was surmounted with a model of Westminster Abbey, exact in every detail, but it is not known if this was one of the clocks on offer.

Another violin made by Charlie Elworthy is still owned by a member of the family; Fred Elworthy of Bickle Farm, Swimbridge. His son Colin told me that all of Charlie's brothers were after it, so he set a price on it, saying the first to come up with the money could have it. Two of Charlie's brothers, Frederick and Ernest, were also first class shots. They were marksmen in the Devon Yeomanry and members of their rifle team.

The Exmoor Rifle Club soldiered on for a few years after Charlie Elworthy's death and was finally disbanded in 1958.

In *The Heritage of Exmoor* I set down the story of the Rev. George Wardropper Surtees, who, without doubt, was the most controversial vicar ever to set foot on Exmoor. In the course of his 27 years sojourn, 1918-1944, he succeeded in antagonising a considerable proportion of the local inhabitants; so much so, that by the mid-1920s a large body of parishioners had broken away from the established church and began holding their own services, first in the open air and later in Frank Vigars' large kitchen at the Post Office. On special occasions Lord Fortescue allowed them the use of his racquets court* at Simonsbath Lodge.

In 1929, an Undenominational Church—Gospel Hall—was erected on a site given by Lord Fortescue adjoining the lane into the school and what is now the car park. It was completed at a cost of £150 and had seating capacity for 50 worshippers.

One of the issues leading to the break away from the established church was the litigation arising out of the transfer of school funds amounting to £83 when the old Board of Managers was disbanded—following the handing over of the school by Lord Fortescue in 1925 to the Somerset County Council Education Authority—to a new Board of School Managers. The

---

* Built in the early 1920s

Rev. Surtees sought to recover this money for the use of the church as he believed the school was a church school, which it was not, although it had been let to the church and run by them for the past 22 years. In this instance the vicar lost the day and the new Board of Managers was allowed to keep the funds. It was decided this money would be used to pay the travelling expenses of special instructors brought in to teach the children of the school extra curricular subjects such as cooking and sewing, gardening and dairy work.

Further legal proceedings were instituted by the Rev. Surtees in 1928 when, following the decision of the Education Authorities to replace the headmistress of the school, Mrs Lena White, with a qualified teacher, and to dispense with the services of the assistant teacher Miss Wilminshurst because of a decline in pupil numbers, the Board of School Managers, led by Lord Fortescue and backed by the majority of the parishioners, decided to present Mrs White with the furniture of the schoolhouse, which she had long enjoyed, as a parting gift in token of their appreciation of her 30 years of dedicated service at the school, in which she had given every satisfaction, both to the School Managers and pupils.

Despite a warning from the Rev. Surtees to the School Managers that they had no right to give away the schoolhouse furniture, they went ahead with the presentation, and the vicar felt duty-bound to take them to court, but just before the case was due to be heard, the issue was settled privately, with the Rev. Surtees agreeing to accept £25 in respect of the value of the furniture and cost of the action. This was borne equally by George Molland for the School Managers, and Mrs Lena White, the innocent recipient of the well intentioned if unfortunate choice of gift.

In the light of ongoing research, further information has come my way, and though it does nothing to alter my opinion of the vicar and his actions, it does reveal that the situation at Simonsbath was much more complicated than first thought.

The Rev. Surtees—a former solicitor—was by nature a blunt and forthright man, who appears to have little consideration for anyone else's point of view, unless it happened to coincide with his own, which did little to endear him to his parishioners, but how much of the antagonism that arose against him was the result of the vicar's nature, and how much of it the result of provocation from a small faction within the village who were determined to make his life a misery, is not easy to decide. It is a little bit like: which came first, the chicken or the egg?

What is known is that within a short time the situation got completely out of hand, and the vicar, believing that nearly everyman's hand was against him, retaliated by threatening litigation against all and sundry; in some cases over the most trivial of matters, which turned even more of his parishioners against him.

One example of the Rev. Surtees' inability to see the other person's point of view involved Jack Little—Mag's father—who for a time rented the Glebe from the vicar, on which to keep a few sheep of his own. All went well until the vicar decided he wanted Jack to build a wall across one of his fields, for which he was quite prepared to pay him, but as Jack tried to tell him, it was more than his job as a shepherd on the estate was worth to be caught working for the vicar in this manner. In consequence, Jack Little lost the ground he was renting and was forced to sell his sheep. He promptly took Mag—who for the past two or three years had been housekeeper at the Vicarage—away from her job, which at that time was worth £15 a year all found; and Jack's wife, who worked part time for the vicar, doing his washing and baking cakes and apple pies, also gave up her job.

Two of the Rev. Surtees' most determined persecutors were taken to court and sued for slander. An undated, unsigned letter to Lord Fortescue, discovered in the Fortescue Archives—in which misconduct by the vicar with one of his parishioners is alleged—undoubtedly concerns this action. Certainly the allegations were in part true; a certain lady in the village did on a number of occasions stay overnight at the vicarage, which the vicar should have realised was bound to set tongues wagging; him being a single man, but that is not to say that anything improper took place, and in order to clear his name he was left with no choice other than to resign—as had been called for—or to take his accusers to court. He chose the latter course of action and won the day, and in the process bankrupted one of his opponents. It made little difference; the bankrupt carried on farming in his wife's name and at every opportunity continued to harass the vicar.

Still the Rev. Surtees soldiered on, though most of his former congregation were now in regular attendance at the Gospel Hall on Sundays. Efforts were made to forget the past and start afresh but there was no increase in numbers at the parish church until after the Rev. Surtees left Exmoor.

In May 1942, after many letters had passed to and from the Diocesan Board at Wells, the Rev. Surtees was offered the position of priest-vicar in the cathedral at Wells, but although he appears to have been on the point of accepting, nothing materialised, and it was not until July 1944 that he tendered his resignation—on health grounds—of the living of the parish of Exmoor and much to the relief of most of his parishioners, finally packed his bags and moved on.

Of one thing we can be certain. The normal happy relationship between the inhabitants of Simonsbath and Exmoor and their vicar; rudely interrupted during the Rev. Surtees' term of office, was quickly re-established when the next vicar, the Rev. Sydney Kell was inaugurated into the living in December, 1944. He expressed his pleasure at the cordial reception he and his wife had received from the parishioners.*

In 1946, when the parish of Exford was without a vicar, Lord Fortescue wrote to the Bishop of Wells suggesting that the amalgamation of the parishes of Exmoor and Exford under one vicar would be a good thing, as he did not think that Exmoor with four farms and twelve cottages and two hotels in Simonsbath, and a few isolated farms on the Moor, warranted a

* Vestry Minutes Book

full time vicar. In the same letter he thoroughly recommended the Rev. Kell for the post should the decision to amalgamate be made, as the vicar was very popular in Exford, having taken the services there since the death of the last vicar. Lord Fortescue expressed his fears that if the amalgamation of the two parishes did not take place, that Exmoor would lose the Rev. Kell.

It was some time before the Bishop—who had only recently been appointed—came to a decision, which was that as Exford could support its own vicar, and there was no legislation at that time whereby a vicar could hold the two posts, it should continue as it was. Shortly after, just as Lord Fortescue had forseen, the Rev. Kell, tendered his resignation, and on 1st January, 1947 took up an appointment as chaplain to the R.A.F.

CHAPTER 8

MEMORIES OF SIMONSBATH, BEFORE, DURING AND AFTER THE SECOND WORLD WAR

IN FOLLOWING the lives and fortunes of some of the inhabitants of Simonsbath we have inevitably gone ahead of other important events and landmarks in the history of the village, and so, before moving on to more recent times it is necessary to turn the clock back a few years in order to bring the rest of our history up-to-date.

Lord Fortescue, the 4th Earl—for whom as Viscount Ebrington the 3rd Earl purchased the Exmoor and Brendon Estates—died in 1932 at the age of 79, only a few days after a major operation. His wife—Countess Fortescue—predeceased him. She died in 1929, some five years after she had been seriously injured as a result of having been thrown while driving her pony and trap at Castle Hill. Although to some extent she recovered from her injuries, she never regained her former good health.

For a few years before he succeeded to the title in 1905, the Earl—as already noted—resided with his wife and children at their Simonsbath Lodge, and thereafter spent part of each year at the Lodge during the hunting season; hunting being one of the very few recreational pastimes his Lordship indulged in, having for a few years from 1881-1887 been the Master of the Devon and Somerset Stag Hounds.

While living at Simonsbath it had been Countess Fortescue's custom to play the organ in church on Sundays, and for a few years prior to her death she provided an annual treat at Castle Hill for the children of Exmoor and Filleigh; a custom that was continued by the 5th Earl and his wife.

The death of the 4th Earl brought to a close an important chapter in the history of Exmoor, particularly where Simonsbath was concerned. Under his direction the village had been enlarged and many improvements made. He had increased the number of smallholdings within the village and provided sustained employment for a considerable workforce, even through the depression of the late 1920s and early 30s. In 1931 Lord Fortescue was still employing 2 horsemen, 9 general labourers, 2 carpenters, a mason and labourer on the Exmoor Estate, most of whom lived in the village, and a further 8 shepherds in outlying farms and cottages on the Moor; also a number of other workers on a part-time basis as and when needed.

As a long term measure to help the unemployed in the Exmoor Region at this time, a major road widening scheme was introduced by the Somerset County Council in 1929 to widen the road from Winsford through Exford to Simonsbath, and on to the county boundary at Brendon Two Gates. The road widening was done in fits and starts as the money became available. The first contractors were forced to pull out when they found they could not do the work for the price they had tendered.

Work in the Simonsbath area commenced at Brendon Two Gates, widening the road towards the village. It provided a useful additional income to many of the smallholders, most of whom had a horse and butt, which were kept busy hauling stone for the roadmaking.

In the early 1930s the line of the main road below the Exmoor Forest Hotel was altered to its present position nearer the river. At the same time improvements were made to the Challacombe road junction and the sharp bend below Simonsbath Barton eased.

It was at this time too that the rather unsightly buildings along the eastern side of the road below those almost opposite the hotel—now being converted into a dwelling house by David Little—were swept away, along with Mary Elworthy's petrol pumps and the stables belonging to the hotel, and the postman's hut. The range of demolished buildings, which served the old Post Office smallholding, were replaced by a single stone built building set back from the road. The petrol pumps were moved across the road and resited above the hotel, and a new stable block erected close by.

The postman's hut was not replaced as by this time it had gone out of use, probably because the Post Office Authority had come to the conclusion that the mail van driver would be bettter employed delivering mail to the outlying farms and cottages rather than hang about in the village for hours until it was time to leave with the outgoing mail. This resulted in two of the three Simonsbath-based postmen losing their jobs, and the duties of the remaining postman were reduced to delivering mail within the village and out along the Challacombe road as far as Cornham Farm.

Frank Vigars, son of the Simonsbath Post Master and estate mason, was one of the postmen to lose his job.[1] He told me he was taken on shortly after he left school in 1924, when a daily moorland postal service was introduced.

Postie Jones did two rounds, alternating them on a day-to-day basis. Postie continued on in the same manner, with Frank alternating likewise.

The two rounds covered a considerable area, and because of the nature of the land in between the remote farms and cottages a pony was found to be the most suitable form of transport, as a result of which Postie Jones became the most photographed postman in the Exmoor region as he went around on his daily 'Pony Express' postal deliveries; one round taking in Kinsford, Emmett's Grange, Wintershead, Horsen, Picked Stones, Honeymead, Winstitchen and Wheal Eliza Cottage; the other—Blackpits, Toms Hill, Larkbarrow, Warren and Gallon House.

The third post-round based at Simonsbath took in the village, Bale Water, Cornham, Pinkery, Driver, Titchcombe, Duredon and Limecombe. For many years this round was done by William Lavercombe, and then by his daughter Frances, but after the mail van took over the outlying farms and cottages the only postman retained was Postie Jones, who then did the village post-round for many years.

In the early 1940s Postie was badly injured in an accident while working on his smallholding, when a set of harrows, pulled by a young newly broken

Road widening near Simonsbath 1931. Group L. to R. Phillips (Exford)
W. Webber (Bridgetown) G. Curtis, B. Tame, chargehand (Exford),
W. Leworthy, P. Doyle (Bridgetown), T. Land (Withypool).

The Old Post Office shortly before demolition in 1938.

Pound Cottages (Lower House) after demolition of Old Post Office, late 1930's.

The Gospel Hall. (Back row) Kempton Jones, Raymond Hunt, Jack Buckingham. (Front row) Stan Curtis, Harold Hunt.

horse, went over him, leaving him with an almost useless arm. He had done very little work on his smallholding beforehand. He did none thereafter, leaving that to his long-suffering wife, who, since their marriage in 1928, had done most of the work on the farm. Postie was, however, able to continue his post round, and did not retire until about 1950 when he was 70 years of age. The cottage and smallholding he had been renting since 1921 was given in up in 1958 when his wife Mary died. He then moved to Bridgwater to live with his son. He died there two years later at the age of 80. His body was brought back to Simonsbath for burial.

For about three years after Postie Jones' retirement the village post round was done by Frank Vigars, the Simonsbath Post Master. On his own retirement in 1953, mail deliveries in the village were undertaken by George Winzer of Exford and then by his brother Gerald. He was followed by Brenda Watts, who in turn was succeeded by Phyllis Prout, and lastly by Gordon Coward, who carried on until this round, too, was taken over by the mail van driver.

Further road widening was carried out in Simonsbath in 1939, along the Challacombe road, at which time the top leat to the sawmill—which had not been used since the turn of the century—was filled in.

Following Mrs Lena White's decision to retire as headmistress of Simonsbath school in 1928, the post was advertised. Shortly after, an interview was held at the school, but the day being very wet only one of the applicants—Miss Olive Badger—turned up.

Raining it may have been, but this did not stop the old Earl from riding over from Castle Hill to take his place with the other school managers for the interview, after which, Miss Badger, a fully qualified teacher with an additional teacher's certificate for school gardening, was offered the position, which she agreed to accept subject to a water supply being piped to the house, which was agreed.

As a result of her experiences during the six years or so she remained at the school, Miss Badger wrote a book called *Transformation*, published by Hodder and Scott-Snell. This book, a novel, was in part factual where her experiences at the school were concerned, but according to Miss Badger the remainder of the book was entirely fictitious. Maybe so, but to those with a good knowledge of Simonsbath at that time, and the ability to read between the lines, it is obvious that parallels have been drawn with real people and actual events, although the names have been changed and the story line altered in much the same way as A. G. Bradley did in his *Exmoor Memories*.

Miss Badger's description of the schoolhouse and school as she found it when first she came to Simonsbath, and incidents at the school while she remained there, are of some interest to students of the history of Exmoor, and as such are described briefly here as follows:

The schoolhouse was a one storey building under the same roof as the school, with low doors and small windows, thick walls and lofty ceilings, no two of which were alike in shape. There was a fair-sized sitting room, whose only pretentions to a fireplace were a couple of iron bars about a foot and a half above the ground. Two small windows in this room, about 1ft square in the middle of the wall each side of the door leading into the schoolroom, were presumably spy windows and relics of a bygone supervision. The next room, which was small, contained a cooking stove. There was one small window in this room, which was placed in such a way that as little light as possible was able to penetrate into the room. Adjoining this room was a fairly good bedroom with an interesting ceiling.

Retracing her steps through the last two rooms, Miss Badger entered a tiny scullery with a door to the outside of the schoolhouse. To the right of the scullery was another small but quite pleasant bedroom with two windows. There was at this time no sink or water laid on indoors, the water having to be fetched from a well 50 yards beyond a plank bridge over the stream (Ashcombe Water). The well water, the finest on the Moor was always cold and never ran dry.*

On entering the schoolroom on her first day as schoolmistress, Miss Badger found it full of smoke; the cleaner told Miss Badger it was always like this, but would clear when the windows and doors were opened. Presently the children dashed in, threw their dinner bags on the floor under the table and darted out again, much to her annoyance, but she smiled when she went out in the playground to call them in. Most of the children had tramped, one, two or three miles to school over hill and dale; many of them did not attend school until they were 7, 8 and even 9, and some, who were outside the three mile limit never went to school at all.

One day while in school the sound of the hunting horn was heard and the older boys pricked up their ears in excitement. Miss Badger turned to write something on the blackboard and the boys slipped out. She rushed out to call them back, but all she saw was the tails of galloping horses and the boys, now mere specks in the distance. On their return the boys were warned that if they did it again they would be punished. Shortly after, the same boys were missing when the staghounds met in the village and were all caned and made to apologise. There was no trouble thereafter. Miss Badger entered the incident in the School Log Book. Lord Fortescue—the 4th Earl—was much amused when he read the report.

On talking to some of the older Simonsbath inhabitants it would appear that the boys had always taken off after the hounds in Mrs White's time when they were in the vicinity, and it was not unknown for some of the girls to chase after them as well.

Rain or shine, the children turned up at school, only severe snowstorms stopping them. After a particularly heavy rainstorm one morning when the children arrived at school soaking wet, with nothing to change into, Miss Badger sent letters off to friends of the school to see if she could raise some money to provide a change of clothes and footwear. As a result of her letters, cheques arrived, enabling the purchase of a change of stockings and shoes for each pupil. The pupils then made bags in which to keep them, and

* This well was destroyed at the time of the Lynmouth Flood

each child had his own peg on which to hang it. Miss Badger also asked Charlie Rich, the blacksmith, if he would make her a boot-track for the children, which he obligingly did.

On the first visit by H. M. Inspector of Schools following Miss Badger's appointment, he was much impressed by the standard of education so far achieved, and on leaving asked her if there was anything she needed. Miss Badger reeled off a list of her requirements—a big tank for water for the school as there was none at hand; a new stove and new desks. The tank and new desks quickly arrived but it was some time before a new stove was fitted. The desks were of solid oak and three girls were assigned to polish them each Friday.

In the course of time Miss Badger introduced music and dancing at the school and an annual play was put on for the benefit of the inhabitants of the village. Woodwork and other crafts wre also introduced, and gardening, which had for many years been on the school curriculum, really flourished after Lord Fortescue allowed them the use of a larger plot of land.

As there was practically no garden to the schoolhouse Miss Badger also asked his Lordship if he would allow her the private use of a piece of land adjoining the house. This was agreed at a nominal rent. The plot contained six huge beech trees and many other smaller trees and shrubs, set in the midst of a perfect wilderness of weeds and brambles. With the help of a couple of workmen and her senior boys the jungle was cleared, paths made, and earth moved to make flower beds, with a star shaped bed for flowers cut by a friendly neighbour. Lord Fortescue was most impressed when next he visited her.

In her book, Miss Badger often refers to her little maid, who in fact was not so little, being 5ft 10in in height. She is not mentioned by name, but was Miss Maberley, a senior girl at her previous school, who remained with her for several years.

A regular visitor to the school was a dear old lady in her eighties, who enjoyed hobnobbing with all and sundry, and though she too is not mentioned by name she was Mrs Jerram, the wife of Charles Samuel Jerram of Talland, Cornwall—who is said to have been a niece of Sir Frederic Knight, but was in fact a second cousin; the daughter of Edward Knight, a son of John Knight's brother Thomas.

It was as a child that Mrs Jerram first came to Simonsbath to stay with Sir Frederic, and one of her diversions at that time was to take the dogs over the moors, and after luring some of the children out of school on some pretence or other, they used to spend the rest of the afternoon trying to lasso rabbits.

At a later date, Mrs Jerram used to bring her children to Simonsbath with her. Three of her children, Charles Frederic, Rowland Christopher, and Cecil Bertrand, later carved out distinguished careers for themselves in the Royal Marines, the Navy and Foreign Service respectively. The latter two sons were knighted for services to their country. Later still, Mrs Jerram brought her grandchildren along, staying at the Exmoor Forest Hotel. For several years it was her custom to present prizes to the children at Simonsbath School, and on a number of occasions she took them off for a school treat.

On the first of such occasions after Miss Badger came to Simonsbath, the children, accompanied by their teacher and Mrs Jerram, set off for the seaside with buckets and spades and balls for games, all provided by their generous benefactor, but on arriving at their destination the children were unusually quiet and ill at ease. Miss Badger quckly realized what was wrong and whispered to the old lady, who with a smile gave the children permission to leave them to go to the shops to spend the few pennies they had saved and brought with them, on the understanding they would return by 12 o'clock for lunch. Many of the children had never been outside their own village before, and such a golden opportunity was not to be missed; all bought something for someone at home.

On a later treat in the summer of 1936, Mrs Jerram took the children to Lynmouth and out for a boat trip. The last recorded occasion she visited Simonsbath was in December 1937, to present prizes at the school. Mrs Maria Florence Jerram died on January 27th 1939 at the age of 85; she is buried in the churchyard at Talland Bay, close by her home for nearly 50 years.

In 1934, only 16 months after the 5th Earl Fortescue succeeded to the title, a disastrous fire, in which two servants died, swept through the mansion at Castle Hill. For the next few years while the house was built rebuilt, Lord Fortescue and his family lived at their Lodge in Simonsbath.

Lady Margaret—Lord Fortescue's eldest daughter—has fond memories of those days and of how she and her brother and sister and cousins ran wild there. The children of the village were, perhaps, a little less enthusiastic about having Lord Fortescue in semi-permanent residence among them, having had it drummed into them by their parents to be always on their best behaviour, and to be mindful of their P's and Q's if spoken to by his Lordship; so much so that when the occasion did arise, one or two of the village children were no longer capable of giving a coherent reply to a simple question. It was not only the children of Simonsbath and Exmoor who were a little afraid of Lord Fortescue: his children also; Lady Margaret tells me it was by no means unknown for her father to chastise his children if he considered they had stepped out of line.

The Fortescue family were still living in Simonsbath when King George V celebrated his Silver Jubilee. To mark the occasion Earl and Countess Fortescue entertained the school children to tea and sports—with prizes—and gave each child a choice Jubilee mug.

With the completion of the rebuilding of the Castle Hill Mansion, Lord Fortescue and his family returned home, but like his father before him continued to spend part of each summer at their Lodge at Simonsbath.

After nearly 20 years in the hotel business Jack and Mary Elworthy retired in March 1936, although Jack still retained some of the land he had been farming. Three years earlier, on 5th April 1933, Jack had applied for and was granted a full licence for the Exmoor Forest Hotel; the licence since 1870 having been for wine only. On giving up the hotel Jack and Mary moved back into their former home at Lower House; Mary's brother William Watts and his wife Mabel moving to Triscombe on the Quantocks, where for 12 months they ran the Blue Ball Inn. While they were living at the inn Mabel's health deteriorated, so they gave it up and returned to Simonsbath, living for a short time with their son Eric, who had married Gwen Elworthy, daughter of William of Duredon in 1933 and was now living at No. 4 West Cottages. Shortly after, William and Mabel moved back into Lower House, which after more than 60 years in single occupation, reverted to two cottages as it had originally been, with William and his wife sharing the premises, and the work on the farm, with Jack and Mary Elworthy.

In 1938, Mary Elworthy—a keen businesswoman who over the years had acquired several properties in North Molton—bought Kinsford, a smallholding close to the Somerset-Devon border on the Simonsbath-South Molton road. She sold a half acre plot there, adjoining the road, to her brother for £26, and William then had a wooden bungalow constructed on this site at a cost of £350. On completion, William and his wife moved in.

When Harry Watts, another of Mary Elworthy's brothers, gave up Horsen Farm in 1942, he and his wife returned to Simonsbath, and they too shared Lower House until 1944, taking over the whole of the premises and the smallholding when Jack and Mary retired and moved to South View, following the death of Charlie Rich. Mary died in 1947, her husband in 1953, and so, after 100 years, the male line of the Elworthy family in Simonsbath—and on Exmoor—ended, as Jack's brother William of Duredon, predeceased him in 1945, and his cousin, Charlie Elworthy, in 1950.

In the last few years of Jack Elworthy's life, following the death of his wife, he was looked after by his brother William's widow, Lucy Elworthy, who, three years or so after Jack's death, moved into Lower House, sharing it first with Harry Watts, and after his death in 1958, with her brother Harry Bond. Lucy lived in what was described in the Exmoor Estate Rent Roll as North Lower House; her brother in South Lower House, in exactly the same way that Thomas Elworthy and Joseph Steer had lived side by side in the same cottages for many years at a much earlier date.

There was another member of the Watts family living in Simonsbath in the 1930s. He was Sidney George Watts,—George—who was a cousin to Mary Elworthy and William and Harry Watts. George worked as a general labourer and rabbit trapper on the estate. He also enjoyed quite a,reputation as a fisherman, though not in the legitimate sense of the word.

George Watts lived in a little hut adjacent to the main road and lane leading down to the farm buildings and river meadows that went with Lower House, though 'lived' is not perhaps the right word, as most of his free time was spent in the Exmoor Forest Hotel. One morning in October 1935, when George had not been seen around the village at his usual time, villagers went to his hut to see if he was alright, only to find him dead in his bunk. He was only 47.

Jack and Mary Elworthy's successor at the Exmoor Forest Hotel was Ernest

Norrish, who had married one of Mary's nieces. By this time the old petrol pumps that had served the villages and visitors so well for the past 20 years or so, were rusted out, so Ernest replaced them with a single hand operated pump, which was tended for many years at a later date by Harry Bond, after he semi-retired when his former employer, William Elworthy, gave up Duredon Farm. Harry also did odd jobs in and around the hotel. He was succeeded by Joe Barwick, former Whipper In with the Exmoor Foxhounds at Bale Water, who, in the process of shooting a fox one day, managed to blow away one of his kneecaps, which incapacitated him somewhat and he was forced to give up his job, as he could no longer ride a horse. While working at the hotel, Joe lodged with Will and Dor Little; first at Little Crocombe and later at West Cottages. Joe died in 1982, and with his death the petrol pump went out of use.

Shortly after Ernest Norrish took over the hotel he installed an electric lighting plant there, giving the hotel an independent supply. This enabled an extension of the old supply at the sawmill to be made to Red Brick House, or Hillcrest as it became known after George Molland, the Exmoor Estate Bailiff for 44 years, died in December in 1936 and was succeeded by John Purchase.

As noted earlier, the old Post Office and cottage adjoining were demolished in 1938. The last person to live in the latter cottage—which for a time in the early part of this century was known as Pitt Cottage—was Mrs Emily Gould, a widow, who was Jack Elworthy's sister. She had taken over the cottage when Seymour Watts moved on.

Taking stock of the inhabitants of Simonsbath during the period between the death of the 4th Earl Fortescue in 1932, and the outbreak of the Second World War in 1939, does not reveal any significant changes to the list of long familiar names within the village. One newcomer to Simonsbath—though not to Exmoor—was George Thorne, whose family had been farming at Emmetts Grange for many years. George, who married one of George Molland's two daughters—his brother Chris, the other—took the tenancy of the Barton in 1935, following William Gammin's retirement.

Another newcomer to Simonsbath who had been living and working on Exmoor for some years was Harry Prout. He came to Exmoor from North Molton in 1922 at the age of 21. For a short time he worked for Chris Thorne at Emmetts Grange before moving on to Warren to work for Tom Elworthy. It was while Harry was at Warren that Tom bought a car, which he apparently had no intention—or inclination—to drive himself, so Harry was shown where the controls were and how they worked. He took to driving like a duck to water, chauffeuring his boss about as and where needed. Harry is believed to have been the first ordinary farmworker on Exmoor to drive a car.

In 1925, when Tom Elworthy moved to Honeymead, Harry went with him. In 1934, Harry married Margaret—Mag—Little, Jack's daughter. The first years of their married life were spent in the cottage that went with Wintershead Farm, which Harry's brother, Will Prout, was then farming. After his marriage Harry worked three days a week for his brother and three days for Thomas Elworthy, and continued to do so until the latter's retirement in 1939, whereupon his brother offered him full time employment, but Mag was not too happy about this suggestion, as Will Prout was not in the habit of paying a regular weekly wage, but paid up when he got around to it, which was no good to Mag trying to run her home, so she persuaded Harry to apply for a vacancy for a general farm worker which had just arisen on the Exmoor Estate, which he did. He got the job, and shortly after, on Lady Day 1939, they moved into No. 2 West Cottages; Horseman George Webber, the former occupant, having now moved to Rose Cottage.

The severe winter of 1938/39, when heavy snowfalls blocked all roads into Simonsbath and it was possible to walk for miles without seeing a hedge, resulted in heavy sheep losses on Exmoor. The winter of 1939/40 was no better. In January 1940 the roads were again blocked with snowdrifts 6-12 feet deep and anything required within the village had to be backpacked in. It was bitterly cold; the moisture in the air froze solid around every twig and branch, breaking them down. Thirty telegraph poles between Simonsbath and Exford were brought down by the sheer weight of ice that had built up around the wires, and the roads were glassy sheets of ice.

By this time we were of course at war with Germany, and virtually the whole of the Exmoor region had been commandeered as one large training area for troops stationed on and around the Moor. The winter was hardly conducive to the success of exercises held there; nevertheless, within a month of the scene described above—which was recorded in the Simonsbath Church Log Book—a major troop exercise on the Moor is described in the same book, under the heading of 'Battle of Exmoor', in which Simonsbath, along with other moorland villages within a radius of 10-15 miles, were positions to be taken or defended.

The exercise was spread over two weeks, with Simonsbath occupied first by an offensive army, and then relieved. Thousands of troops of every description, with convoys of buses, lorries and guns passed through the village in all directions. All went well until someone, somewhere, gave a wrong order, and within a very short time every road leading into Simonsbath was blocked solid and traffic brought to a complete standstill.

The first part of the exercise was held in continuous pouring rain, the second was severely disrupted by a heavy snowstorm which lasted 24 hours, and sadly ended in tragedy. Hundreds of men in widespread positions out on the Moor, encumbered with vehicles, medium range guns, small arms and other equipment, which could not be moved, quickly realised the danger they were in, and, having consumed such rations as they had, abandoned their positions, leaving most of their equipment behind in snow 2-3 feet deep. The troops then made their way to the nearest road. By the time they reached it many were exhausted, and were revived only by the hospitality of nearby farms and cottages. It is believed seven men probably died. At least three of them were killed by the fumes of a lorry in which they had taken shelter and kept the engine running for warmth. None of those who died were buried at Simonsbath.

In the early days of the following week, relays of troops, mainly from the camp at Torrington, came to Exmoor to recover the vehicles, guns, etc., abandoned on the moors. Thus ended the only Battle of Exmoor known to history.

The Battle of Exmoor was followed in July 1940 by an invasion of evacuees, 23 boys and 7 girls from Goodall Road School, Leyton, who were accompanied by their teacher Mr Frank Betts.* A week later, when all the children had been settled in their new homes, an evacuee school was set up in the Gospel Hall, or Meeting House as it was now known. The village school was amalgamated with the evacuee school in 1942, with the Meeting House retained as a second classroom.

Two other schools were established in the village during the war, both of them in Simonsbath Lodge. The first was a private girls school, which remained there for three or four years. This was followed by a private boys school whose term of residence there was of even shorter duration.

A number of wartime incidents were recorded in the Simonsbath School Log Book. Gas masks were issued to the 20 children attending the school in May 1940. In June the same year, Mrs Walker, who had taken over from Mrs Marshall (Miss Badger's successor) in 1938, set the children to work catching Cabbage White butterflies of which there was a plague that year. In a very short time the children had caught 592, and Mrs Walker noted in the log book that from that time on she would buy these butterflies dead at the rate of 1d for 50. Mrs Walker's interest in the death of the Cabbage White butterfly does seem a little odd, seeing as how gardening was no longer on the school curriculum. This had been discontinued when Mrs Marshall took over from Miss Badger, and was not renewed during the five years that Mrs Walker remained at the school. Gardening was re-introduced by Miss Barralet shortly after she became headmistress in 1944, with the help of Mr Cripps, who had been appointed earlier to teach the senior class. By this time the gardens used by Miss Badger and her pupils had been taken back into the estate farm, and new gardens were made in the small field behind Simonsbath Lodge and the shelter belt of trees, where a number of villagers had their plots.

The arrival of the evacuee children in Simonsbath, and their subsequent placement in cottages in the village and farmhouses out on the Moor, had one beneficial effect as far as the children living way out on Exmoor were concerned. For over 80 years children had made their way to school as best they could, mostly on foot; one or two on ponies, which were left in the old stables at White Rock—adjacent to the schoolhouse—during school hours. Now, with the arrival of the evacuees, a school car service was laid on for the benefit of all children out on the Moor. It is, perhaps, ironic that in a time of war when there was an acute petrol shortage in this country that such a service should have been provided. Of one thing we can be certain; had there been no evacuees, there would have been no transport provided for the

* He resided at No. 5, West Cottages for the duration of the war

local boys and girls, who would have continued to make their way to school as best they could.

William Watts, long time taxi driver for Mary Elworthy at the hotel, now living at Dunmoor, Kinsford, provided the first car service on Exmoor with his own car. The inaugural journey was made on 22nd July 1940, collecting children from Kinsford, Emmetts Grange, Wintershead and Horsen.

Twelve months later, an entry in the School Log Book reveals that William had exhausted his petrol allowance and could not bring the children to school until the situation was resolved. The problem must have been sorted out fairly quickly because William was certainly back in business in September and October, with mileage returns of 492 and 420 recorded respectively.

There were a number of other occasions when William Watts could not make the journey to Simonsbath, particularly in winter when there was snow and ice about; and one day, just before the war ended, nine children failed to make it to school when a large aeroplane was forced down on the road between Kinsford and Blue Gate, blocking the road to the village.

A number of other Royal Air Force planes crashed on Exmoor during operational duties; one of which—a Wellington bomber—badly damaged the west end cottage at West Gate. Alfie Barwick, who was then living in the cottage with his mother, was in bed at the time, and was buried by the debris. His mother at first thought he was dead as the crash didn't waken him, but he escaped unscathed. She had a further shock when she looked out of the window, straight at the lifeless body of the pilot who had stayed with his plane. The rest of the crew had all baled out and landed safely. One, who turned up at Aclands, had no idea where he was, and was most relieved to find he had landed on English soil.

A propeller from the plane was picked up by Brian Walker, the young son of the village schoolmistress, and taken home to the schoolhouse. When the Walker family left Simonsbath, Brian buried the propeller close by. As far as is known it is still where he buried it.

Not all of the evacuee children who came to Simonsbath survived the war. Two, a brother and sister, aged between seven and ten, who should never have been parted, were split up. Mag had the little girl, the boy was placed at Warren Farm, miles away. The children were most unhappy and wrote to their mother, who came down to take them home. All were killed in a bombing raid on London. Two more children were also taken home by their mother, who missed their company. She said it was better to be bombed then bored. Sadly her words came true, and they too were all killed.

There was much stricter rationing on Exmoor during the Second World War, and though no one went hungry there was little food to spare when social evenings, dances, whist drives etc., were held in the village, where formerly a scrumptious spread was always provided. During the war—and after—most of these functions were held in the Tea Room, which was built in the grounds of the Exmoor Forest Hotel shortly before the commencement of hostilities, to cater for an increasing number of visitors to Simonsbath. Because of rationing the hotel could provide little by way of refreshments, but it was surprising what could be accomplished with two or three cooked rabbits and a piece of boiled ham from someone's salter. Rabbit and ham, when minced together, make very tasty sandwiches, so Mag was telling me one day when we were reminiscing about life in Simonsbath during the war.

Prior to the turn of the century such functions as were held, were usually held in the schoolroom, and more rarely in the Wool Chamber, but after Viscount Ebrington built his new range of stables and the coach house, he allowed the villagers the use of the latter for special occasions. At this time music was provided by Harry Watts on the violin, and his sister Mary Elworthy on the piano. In the late 1920s after the Racquets Court was built at Simonsbath Lodge, dances and other entertainments were usually held there. At a later date, dances were again held in the schoolroom, and finally in the Tea Room above the Exmoor Forest Hotel.

Bands or groups that used to play regularly in Simonsbath were Bert Robins and his Blue Rhythm Band, consisting of four brothers from the parish of High Bray; also Herbie Slade, a one man band with accordion and foot operated drum, who after the war was joined by his two sons. For Saturday night social evenings, music was provided by Hughie Jones— grandson of Eli—on his accordion, and later, in 1948/49 five local lads formed the Exmoor Accordion Band. The members of this band were Roger Nichols and John James from Exford and Stan Curtis, Raymond and Harold Hunt from the Simonsbath area.

In Mag's younger days, lack of transport was no deterrent to going to dances in other villages on the Moor. Many was the time when Mag and her friends walked the five miles to Exford, danced all night and then walked home again.

If ever the spirit of Exmoor was embodied in the heart and soul of one man, then that man was surely Jack Buckingham, who apart from a couple of short spells in hospital, never spent a night away from his beloved Exmoor. Jack was born at Lower Sherdon Farm on 27th April 1921, the 5th and last generation of his family to live on Exmoor Proper; his ancestors being among the earliest pioneer farming families on Exmoor, originating from Twitchen. Jack's early life was marred by the tragic death of his younger and only brother James, who was swept away and drowned while attempting to cross a swollen stream, Jack, who was with him, being unable to save him. A few years later, in 1936, tragedy struck again when Jack was only 14 and his father died.

In spite of his youth Jack desperately wanted to carry on the farm, but although he had the promise of help and guidance from the Executors of his father's estate—Will Prout and John Ley—his mother was set against the idea, and shortly after let—and later sold—the farm, to Mag's brother Stan Little.

Immediately after the farm was let, Jack left home to go to work for George Thorne at Simonsbath Barton, living in. Two years later, in 1938, he left to take employment on the Exmoor Estate. He was still working on the estate, albeit in a part-time capacity, at the time of his death 50 years later.

*The Exmoor Accordion Band L. to R. Harold Hunt, Stan Curtis,
Johnny James and Roger Nicholls.*

Jack Buckingham.

Archie Little, Author and Margaret (Mag) Prout of Rose Cottage
(sister to Arch).

The Exmoor Forest Hotel, Frank Curtis cleaning up the mess after the
Flood Disaster 1952.

Following his departure from the Barton Jack lodged for a short while with his aunt and uncle, Minnie and Frank Vigars at the Post Office, and then with Bert Jones at Winstitchen, where he was quite happy until he had a slight altercation with a couple of evacuee boys and it was thought best that he should leave. By this time Jack had become friendly with Harry and Mag Prout and he inquired of them if they knew anywhere that he might stay. After Jack was gone, Harry and Mag talked it over and decided that as their evacuee had returned home and they had a spare bedroom, that Jack could have it until such time as he was properly fixed up. Little did they realise that Jack would remain with them until the day he died, but this was the case, for Jack, who never married, continued to live with his friends, not so much as a lodger but as one of the family, first at West Cottages and then at Rose Cottage, watching over Harry and Mag's three children as they grew up, sharing their joys and sorrows. The years passed quickly by; the children left school, took jobs, married, and in their turn had families, who all came to know and love Jack, who was never far away when needed.

n 1939, a year after Jack began work on the estate, the first tractor—a Standard Fordson—was purchased, and Jack, who had a keen interest in all things mechanical, was given the job of driving it. All went well for some years until March 1947, when Jack, while working around the steep cleaves close to where Cornham Bungalow now stands, lost control of his tractor and it rolled over and over down the steep hillside, badly crushing him in the process. Somehow, with several cracked ribs, a punctured lung and a broken nose he managed to crawl home to West Cottages, a mile or so away, where Mag found him in a terrible state, more dead than alive, mud and blood all over. She cleaned him up as best she could and sent for John Purchase, the Estate Bailiff, who quickly arrived and drove Jack to his doctor at South Molton, and from there on to the North Devon Infirmary at Barnstaple, where, after examination, he was transferred to the Orthopaedic Hospital at Exeter. Jack recovered from his injuries but the damage done to his chest and lungs is believed to have been the cause of much suffering and discomfort in later life, and ultimately, his death. A second accident in the same year was less serious, for on this occasion Jack managed to jump off the tractor just before it ended up in a ditch. He was a more cautious man thereafter, and though he continued to drive a tractor for the rest of his life, he would never drive one fitted with a cab; the fear of being trapped inside greatly outweighing the additional comfort it would have brought him.

As time went by and additional tractors were brought into use on the estate farm, Jack began to spend more and more of his time on repairs to the old wall and bank fences erected by the Knight family many years earlier. He became a skilled craftsman, taking a great pride in his work. For many years too he also helped the shepherds at shearing and lambing times. In later years, when the weather was too severe to work on the moor, he assisted in the sawmill. On fine summer evenings and weekends he was often to be found on Buscombe cutting turf (peat) for the home fire at Rose Cottage and for a few of his neighbours; or out on Brendon Common doing the same for Dick French of Brendon Barton. It was largely due to his efforts that this age old custom has survived to the present day on Exmoor.

Although I did not meet up with Jack Buckingham until the mid-1980s, we were instantly at ease with one another and within minutes deep into Exmoor's past history, with Jack as eager to learn from me as I was from him, and for nigh on six hours we talked incessantly. This was but the first of many such meetings. We were fairly evenly matched; my knowledge coming from over 36 years of wandering the length and breadth of Exmoor and several years of intensive research in Record Offices and libraries around the country; Jack's knowledge being the accumulation of a lifetime of living and working on the Moor, which had benefitted from an insatiable curiosity about all aspects of Exmoor history. As a young man he had been able to talk to many of the old inhabitants of Simonsbath and Exmoor, some of them only two generations removed from John Knight's earliest long time employees, and had thus gained an unrivalled knowledge of life on Exmoor that went way back into the last century. Jack also had a countryman's eyes and missed nothing as he went about his daily duties. His memory for detail and dates was incredibly accurate, and with all the documents and information at my disposal I never once found him wrong in anything he told me. If Jack wasn't sure of his facts, he would tell you nothing.

In the all too short time I knew Jack before he died on 13th January 1988, I learned more about Simonsbath and Exmoor and its inhabitants than could be learned in a lifetime of searching through old documents and newspapers. Without his help much of the history of Simonsbath and Exmoor could not have been written, and I will be forever thankful that I was privileged to share his memories in what sadly proved to be the last few years of his life.

The 1940s and 50s took a heavy toll on Simonsbath's long established residents and other familiar faces around the village. John Blackmore passed away in 1940; Charlie Rich 1944; Bill Staddon 1945; Mary Elworthy 1947; Charlie Elworthy 1950; Emily Hunt 1951; Jack Elworthy 1953; William Lavercombe 1954; William Hunt 1958; George Webber (Horseman George) 1959, and Postie Jones in 1960. Others who were associated with the village over a period of many years also passed on. They included William Elworthy in 1945; William Steer 1954; and Harry Watts in 1958.

Harry Watts, who took over Lower House and smallholding in 1944, continued to farm there until 1953 when he sold off all of his farming stock and retired. He continued to live in the cottage almost to the time of his death, following a stroke. For a few years prior to his death he provided the school car service—having taken over when his brother William gave it up—and had driven the children to school on the day he had his stroke.

The death or retirement of so many of the long established tenants of Lord Fortescue's cottage smallholding in Simonsbath had a profound effect on a way of life within the village that had begun a century before. All of the land that formerly went with these holdings—apart from 31 acres of Lower House ground whch was let to Mr J. F. A'Brooke[2]—who was non-resident in the village—and 33 acres leased by the Exmoor Hunt with Bale Water—was taken in hand by the estate.

The late Tom Little of Barnstaple claimed that prior to the granting of a full licence to the Exmoor Forest Hotel in 1933, none of the smallholdings ever lacked a new tenant when they became vacant, but afterwards none were even re-let; implying that this was the prime reason for the lack of interest. Although there is good reason to believe that there was a great deal of truth in his claim, another factor to take into consideration is that as most of the holdings did not become vacant—until the 1940s and 50s, by which time wages had increased considerably—there was less incentive for a man to give up a regular well paid job to go farming on his own account. Moreover, the Exmoor Estate no longer employed the same amount of casual labour as they had in the past; on which the smallholders had relied heavily to make a decent living.

One of the concessions granted to employees on the Exmoor Estate, was that of keeping a cow—two in the case of the shepherds. This custom began to die out about the time of the Second World War, when, because of a tendency towards smaller families, less milk was needed, and where a cow was still kept, it usually produced enough milk to supply one or more neighbours. In the past it was a familiar sight to see the cows belonging to the estate workers—who for the most part lived in West Cottages and at West Gate—being driven along the road to the far side of Limecombe and up on to Big Duredon to graze, and then home again in the evening to be milked, each cow turning into its own shippen. With the advent of a six day a week delivery of milk, the keeping of a cow and the work it entailed was no longer worth the bother, and one by one they were given up.[2]

The demise of that special breed of small farmers in Simonsbath—real characters one and all—was to some extent balanced by a number of new-comers to the village. Ernest Norrish and his wife, who took over the Exmoor Forest Hotel when Jack and Mary Elworthy retired, moved on in 1940, and for the next two years the hotel and land that went with it was rented by a man called Beer. He gave up the hotel in 1942 and moved to Withypool, but retained the land he had been renting for a few years longer. He was the last tenant to rent the hotel and land together.

In the next six years, the tenancy of the hotel changed hands four times. Mrs Brierley—Mr Beer's successor—was gone by 1944; Mr and Mrs Penny by 1946, and Mr Mayger by 1948. He was followed by Mr and Mrs Holman, about whom more will be related later.

Among the other new arrivals in Simonsbath were Leonard Eaton and Harold James, both of whom were employed on the estate; Leonard as a general labourer, and Harold as a carpenter.

In 1938, Leonard Eaton married Winnie (Win) Little—Mag's sister. For two years or so after their marriage they lived at Driver Cot, moving into No. 6 West Cottages in January 1941, following the death of the former occupant, John Blackmore. Leonard and Win could not have chosen a worse day for moving into their new home, as their arrival in Simonsbath coincided with that of a blizzard. It took them days to dry out their belongings. They remained at West Cottages until 1958, when Leonard gave up his job and they moved to Bridgwater.

Harold James' arrival in Simonsbath was less dramatic. He moved into No. 2 West Cottages* shortly after Harry and Mag Prout and their children, along with Jack Buckingham, moved to Rose Cottage in August or September 1947, which they took over from Jack Watts—William's son—who for a short time after he was demobbed from the army, worked on the estate. Jack's predecessor at Rose Cottage, Raymond Lloyd and his wife Winifred— the daughter of a former occupant, Jack (Johnny Socks) Jones, shepherd of Badgworthy and Blackpits—had also been in the services, where they met, fell in love and married. Their stay at Rose Cottage was also of short duration, and was merely a transitional step between leaving the army and moving on to a higher paid position in Coventry, which was the reason why Jack Jones gave up his herding and moved to Coventry with his wife to be near them, though Jack can hardly be said to have advanced his position in life as the only job he could get there was as a gravedigger.

Shortly after Harold James settled in Simonsbath, Mag's mother, Alice Little—Jack's wife—died, and Harold, although a newcomer to the village, offered his services as a bearer; a lovely gesture and one that was much appreciated by the Little family. The funeral service, held on 22nd May 1948, was the first such service conducted by the Rev. Basil Norris, who had been inducted to the living only a few days before. He succeeded the Rev. Kell.

The Rev. Norris, a bachelor, quickly became a much loved and respected member of the Simonsbath and Exmoor community, who mixed well with all classes of society. For the first 12 months or so after he became the Vicar of Exmoor there was no church organist, so he played the organ himself. On visiting Rose Cottage one day he noticed an organ in the living room of the cottage and asked Mag who played it. Mag told him that she did, whereupon he asked her if she would like to be his church organist, which at first Mag was reluctant to do, because although she had picked up the basics of reading music at school, she was entirely self taught as far as playing was concerned, and did not think she was good enough to play in public, but after the Vicar told her he would let her have the hymns and psalms a week beforehand so she would hve plenty of time to practise them, she agreed to play, and did so for the 11 years or so that the Rev. Norris remained the Vicar of Exmoor.

For a short time after the Private Boys School left Simonsbath Lodge it remained empty. It was then let to a Mrs Jeeves who ran it as a private hotel under the name of Diana Lodge Hotel. She also kept horses. Mrs Jeeves was gone and the place again empty when Major John Coleman Cooke—an army colleague of my father, saw it, fell in love with it, and shortly after acquired a lease for it and moved in.

Major Cooke, a Fellow of the Zoological Society, writer, broadcaster and conservationist, was instrumental in founding the Exmoor Society, an

* After Charlie Elworthy's death in 1950, Harold moved into No. 1

amenity group dedicated to the preservation of the natural character of the moorlands and the promotion of all aspects of Exmoor life.

For nearly 20 years, Major Cooke and his wife remained at Simonsbath and three of their four children were born there. When he first came to live at the Lodge Major Cooke took over the whole of the building, but at a later date parts of it were sub-let. The west wing—added by Viscount Ebrington around the turn of the century—was let to a writer, but by 1957 this wing had been taken in hand by the estate as accommodation for an estate worker. He was Frank Curtis, former shepherd at Black Pits, who gave up his herding in 1953 and moved into No. 2 West Cottages with his wife Nell—the eldest of Dick Jones' three daughters—and the rest of his family, moving on in 1957 into the west wing of the Lodge. Although Frank had given up his herding, he had merely swapped one job on the estate for another and was now employed as a general farm labourer, and continued so until 1962, when he gave up his job and moved to Exton.

Some of the upstairs rooms in the central part of the Lodge were also turned into a flat. Hitherto, the main access to the upper floors was via a staircase at the rear of the house, which, with the making of the flat, was not now the most convenient of arrangements, so Major Cooke, with the consent of the Fortescue famly, had the staircase that now leads from the entrance lounge to the upper level, put in. The staircase was made and fixed by Frank Vigars senior, who, although a mason by trade, could turn his hand to anything—his son Frank also.

The first—and only—occupant of the newly erected upstairs flat in the Lodge was a Miss Forman, a keen huntswoman, who besides keeping horses also had two pretty little terriers called Whisky and Soda. Mag, who at that time was working part-time for Major Cooke, undertook to do the same for Miss Forman.

It was around this time that Captain Wallace, who later became the Master of the Exmoor Foxhounds at Bale Water—but was at that time Master of the Heythrop Hunt—began to come to Simonsbath by invitation of the Exmoor Hunt, to hunt the district; the season for hunting in his own area having finished earlier, Captain Wallace and his entourage of huntsman, whipper-in, grooms etc., always stayed at the Exmoor Forest Hotel, and memorable occasions they were too. The hounds were kept in the coach house, and the horses in the stables adjoining.

Major Cooke and his family moved to Braunton in 1968, where he continued to work for conservation, even though his health was deteriorating. He died in a London hospital in 1978 at the age of 64. His ashes were brought back to Simonsbath for interment in the churchyard.

The Lynmouth Flood Disaster of 1952, the worst of its kind ever recorded in this country, emanated on the high ground of Exmoor above Simonsbath, where, after exceptionally heavy rain during the first fortnight in August, which culminated in a torrential downpour on the 15th, the moorland was awash with water several inches deep. Within hours, the streams and rivers of the moor—which were already way above their normal level—became raging torrents, which resulted not only in the destruction of the greater part of the lovely village of Lynmouth, and a tragic loss of life, but also caused severe flooding and considerable damage to properties in many other villages on and around the Moor.

In Simonsbath, the bridge across the River Barle was severely damaged when the water rose suddenly 10-12ft. Later, a Bailey Bridge was placed alongside until such time as the old bridge could be rebuilt.

Scarcely a house within the village escaped flooding. The water level of the stream passing through Ashcombe Bottom, and the tiny rivulet flowing through the grounds of the vicarage rose so quickly that Frank Vigars, the village Post Master, who was working on his shed at the rear of his home at Jubilee Villas, didn't realise there was a problem until he heard his wife screaming. With some difficult he made his way back indoors, just in time to rescue his wife and two grand-daughters, who were floating about in the kitchen, and carry them to the relative safety of his woodshed, where they were joined shortly after by his next door neighbour, Jack Elworthy and his housekeeper, Lucy Elworthy—the widow of his brother William.

Close by, at a slightly lower level, the Exmoor Forest Hotel was flooded almost to ceiling height in the back bar, and was four to five feet deep in the front rooms. Mr Holman and his family, along with about 24 guests staying at the hotel and three or four local residents, took refuge upstairs, where, after talking over the seriousness of the situation, it was decided to try to get downstairs to see if they could reach the front door of the hotel and break it down, to reduce the water level inside. The first attempt by Mr Holman and his two boys failed, the water being too deep, but shortly after, Stan Curtis, his brother Denzil, and brother-in-law Bob Barrow, succeeded in getting through to the front bar, where by climbing out of the top half of a window reached the front door. The panels of the door were then smashed in with a piece of timber; the force of the released pent-up water nearly washing them away, and taking with it the till from the bar and other contents of the hotel, along with coke and coal from the cellars, which was strewn about the meadows adjacent to the Barle and down the lane below Birch Cleave. Much of the coke and coal was later salvaged and returned to the hotel.

Strangely, although Lower House lies below the hotel and was right in the path of the raging torrent, not one drop of water entered the house. Stan Curtis put this down to the fact that the cottage was built on a slightly higher ridge of rock, and though millions of gallons of water were pouring down Ashcombe, this was enough to divert the water away from the cottage, thus saving the inmates from a severe flooding.

At the time the floodwaters were reaching their peak, Mag was away from her home at Rose Cottage, helping out at Honeymead House, where Sir Robert Waley-Cohen was giving a party. The guests had just finished eating, and Mag was clearing up, when water burst through the window at the back of the house. After the water had subsided a little Mag thought it best to make tracks for home, and got as far as the village, where she found

Mr Holman stopping all traffic—vehicular and on foot—as both bridges across Ashcombe Water had been swept away. Mag was, however, able to make her way to Lower House, and remained there with Harry and Lily Watts until Dick Little—Mag's nephew—who had been visiting Jack Buckingham at Rose Cottage, came to find her and help her to reach her home. Dick had found that although both bridges had been swept away, a narrow strip of masonry, all that was left of the higher bridge carrying the back road into Simonsbath Lodge, had remained in place and they were able to cross this safely, to get home.

On reaching home, Mag found that Rose Cottage too had been inundated with floodwater, which had poured off the field above the cottage and built up at the end of the house until a window caved in under the pressure. Jack Buckingham and Mag's husband Harry were doing their best to clean up the mess. Mag then set to work, after first putting her two youngest children Henry and Shirley to bed, but thunder and lightening upset them and Phyllis, their elder sister, was sent upstairs to console them. Outside, the floodwaters had gouged out the pathway beside the cottage, undermining the foundations. A pyrex dish containing food for Shirley's cat, which had been left on the doorstep, was washed away. Dick Little apologised to Mag for being unable to save it. He said 'Sorry, madam, it just went tinkle, tinkle into little pieces'.

Two men, who had been on their way to Lynton and were stopped by the floodwaters at Simonsbath, spent the night at Rose Cottage. They left early the next morning to continue their journey on foot, after thanking Mag for her hospitality, but Bill Kingdom, who worked at Wintershead, who also spent the night at Rose Cottage after being marooned in the village when he came down for a drink, walked out in the morning without so much as a good morning greeting, much less a thank you.

There was also severe flooding along the Challacombe road at West Cottages, and at Westgate, but fortunately, here, as elsewhere in the village, damage was confined to property and there was no loss of life. Five days after the flood—and as a direct result of it—the road at Westgate collapsed, and all traffic westwards to Challacombe ceased forthwith.

The debris brought down by the floodwaters of the River Barle and its tributary streams choked the leat to the sawmill and cut off the electricity supply to the village, but as this only supplied electric lighting this was by no means the worse of calamities.

Although only minor damage was done to the weirs and sluice'gates, and it would not have been a difficult task to restore water power to the mill, the Fortescue Estate decided to dispense with the turbine and replaced it with a Ruston Hornsby heavy oil engine, which provided all the power needed at the sawmill, and continued to generate electricity until the main supply was connected to the village in 1962.

1952, the year of the flood, ended with a blizzard. Simonsbath was again cut off from the outside world, with the roads blocked by huge drifts. It had certainly been an eventful year, and one the villagers were not sorry to see the back of.

CHAPTER 9

THE END OF AN ERA

JOHN Purchase, the Exmoor Estate Bailiff since 1936, retired in 1953. He, like his predecessor George Molland, had carried out his duties in a loyal and conscientious manner, and was also highly regarded by the men in his charge. Only one minor incident marred an otherwise unblemished record. This occurred on a day when John was in a bit of a hurry to get to Cornham Farm, so he decided to take his car, but as he also needed his pony when he got there, he hitched a rope from car to pony and ran it along behind. Unfortunately he was spotted by Mr Liversage—a Special Constable—who for a couple of years or so lived in one of the Westgate Cottages. He reported the matter to his superiors who decided to prosecute, and John Purchase was subsequently fined for the offence.

The next Estate Bailiff was John Hayes, and it was during his term of office—with the aid of government grants—that work was begun on modernising the farmhouses and cottages on the Exmoor Estate. Within the village of Simonsbath an indoor supply of piped water was almost unheard of prior to modernisation; most of the villagers counting themselves lucky if they had a tap fixed to the outside wall of their cottages.

Although the modernisation programme took more than ten years to complete, at the end of the day every estate cottage in the village had the luxury of a bathroom with running hot water; and flush toilets and septic tank drainage replaced the old outdoor bucket closets. Hitherto, the only cottage in the village to boast an indoor flush toilet was No. 1 West Cottages, although this had not been installed by the estate, but by Charlie Elworthy during his occupancy.

As each cottage was modernised, the old Bodley stove—or that of similar type—which had served the villagers so well for many a long year, was done away with and replaced with a Rayburn, which also provided the hot water.

In 1953, the old groom's bothy above George Webber and Bill Staddon's stables, was converted into a dwelling house, although mod cons were not provided at that time. Thereafter, this cottage has been known as Stable Flat; the first occupants of which were Stan Curtis and his wife Millie, who moved in shortly after their marriage.

For some years in his younger days Stan worked on the Honeymead Estate for the Waley-Cohen family, while he awaited a vacancy on the Exmoor Estate. On 6th August 1950 he was taken on as a horseman by the latter estate, working a pair of carthorses, Misty and Farmer, but after their services were dispensed with in 1954, Stan became a tractor driver, and continued so until he retired 38 years later in September 1992; ending up as senior hand.

In February 1956 Stan and Millie moved into Jack and Mary Elworthy's former home at South View (Jubilee Villas) and opened a general store; Mrs Batten who had taken over the Post Office and Stores next door having given up this side of the business. Two years later, on 1st September 1958, the Post Office was also transferred to Stan and Millie.

Mrs Batten and her husband Bill—who had succeeded Frank Vigars as a mason on the estate—continued to live in No. 1 Jubilee Villas until 1963, when they left the village. Incidentally, Mrs Batten was the first person in Simonsbath to have a colour TV set, which was installed shortly after mains electricity was connected to the village in 1962.[1] The first to have black and white television sets in the Simonsbath area were George Thorne at the Barton and Eric Watts at Duredon, in the early 1950s, followed a year or two later by Mag at Rose Cottage. All of these TVs were powered by small portable generating sets and the picture provided was quite acceptable.

Stan and Millie gave up the Post Office and Stores in 1966, which was then taken over by John Watts (Eric's son) and his wife Brenda, who for the past three years had been living in the west wing of the Lodge. The value of the stock taken over when the store changed hands was £376.3.8.

After giving up the Post Office and Stores, Stan and Millie returned to Stable Flat, which since their departure had been occupied by Dennis Little, who had married Miss Forman's groom, Joyce Bunn. Dennis, the eldest son of Will and Dor Little, was taken on by the estate as a general labourer following the completion of his National Service, and like most employees on the estate could have reasonably expected to remain on the payroll until he retired, but it was not to be, for on hearing that Dennis had developed Hodgkins Disease, he was given his notice, which, as might have been expected, did not go down too well with his family and friends.

It was not until after Stan and Millie returned to Stable Flat that it was fitted out with mod cons. This was the last cottage in the village to be modernised by the estate; work at Rose Cottage having been completed a year or so earlier.

In the course of less than 20 years prior to modernisation, which included the installation of a Rayburn and a new chimney, Mag had succeeded in burning out two stoves and setting the chimney on fire a time or two, which to anyone who knows Mag and has experienced the warmth of her kitchen, and suspects that it is her ambition to burn all of the wood on Exmoor before she expires, is not surprising, but it was not all her fault as the old stove in the kitchen had been poorly connected into the sitting room chimney with a short length of pipe, which was a constant source of trouble.

New bungalows were also built. The first, which became known as Little Crocombe, was erected adjacent to the south side of the Simonsbath-Exford highway, about 100 yards or so before the turning into Winstitchen Farm. Little Crocombe was completed in 1951, and first occupied in the following year by the shepherd of the Mines Herding; Will and Dor Little and their family, who since 1939 had been living in the old miner's cottage at Wheal Eliza.

Will and Dor remained at Little Crocombe until 1971, when Will semi-retired and the couple moved into No. 2 West Cottages, from where Will ran a half herding at the Barton almost to the time of his death in October 1982, at the age of 77. Will claimed that he was the longest serving employee on the Exmoor Estate, with an unbroken service of 63 years, which was not quite correct, as for 18 months or thereabouts in the late 1930s, Will and his family lived at Brixham. Nevertheless, 61 years in one employment is still a very impressive record.

Two more bungalows were built for shepherds in 1958/59. One, known as Ashcombe Bungalow, was erected on a plot of land between Little Crocombe and Winstitchen Lane, to serve a new herding created when the herding at Hoar Oak was given up. This bungalow was first occupied by Denzil Curtis—Stan's brother—formerly the shepherd of the Blackpits herding, who had the sad misfortune to lose his wife shortly after the birth of their second child, only two years after they had moved into their new home.

Following the death of Vera Curtis at the age of only 23, her father, Will Hobbs—who was now working on the estate as a general labourer—moved to Ashcombe with his wife to look after Denzil and the children, returning to West Cottages in 1963 after Denzil re-married, though not into their former home at No. 2, but into one of the older cottages, No. 4. In 1969, when Denzil gave up his herding and left the village, Will Hobbs and his wife returned to Ashcombe to take over the herding, which Will retained until his retirement in 1976. The last years of his life were spent in No. 2 Westgate Cottages, where he died in 1984 at the age of 72.

The other new bungalow, known as Cornham Bungalow, which was built to replace the rather remote Titchcombe bungalow, was placed on the hill west of the bridge over Bale Water, south of the kennels and the Simonsbath-Challacombe road. The first application to build there in 1957 by Lord Fortescue, was turned down by the National Park Planning Authority, but was granted on appeal. Bill Land, who was at that time the shepherd of the Titchcombe Herding, was the first to live there.

Two years or so before Cornham Bungalow was built, Bill Westacott, the shepherd of the Limecombe Herding—who since 1947 had been living in Limecombe Cottage—moved into No. 1 West Cottages, which had become vacant after Harold James's successor—a carpenter by the name of Bellingham—had left the village.

Bill Westacott retired in 1962, whereupon he and his wife moved to the White House at Exford, to look after the house and smallholding which George Thorne of Simonsbath Barton had purchased preparatory to his own retirement. In 1969, when George retired, Bill Westacott and his wife returned to Simonsbath, though not into an estate cottage, but into one of the two Council Houses that had been built in 1960/61 on a site between Birch Cleave Wood and Little Crocombe, which the Somerset County Council had acquired from the Exmoor Estate in 1957.* At the time the

---

* Information supplied by Mr Hugh Thomas, Agent to the Fortescue Estates

Council Houses were built there was ample accommodation in the village to meet the needs of the community, so the new houses were let to families from Exford.

Bill Westacott spent his declining years in his new home. He was another of Exmoor's real old characters, who for the price of a pint or two of ale could tell up a fair old tale. He died at the age of 83 in 1980.

It is not proposed here to deal with Bill Westacott's successors as shepherds of the Limecombe Herding, who until very recently all lived in No. 1 West Cottage; nor with the shepherds who lived in the Little Crocombe, Ashcombe and Cornham bungalows, as this subject has been adequately dealt with in *The Heritage of Exmoor* (pages 263-270), so we will now move on to other changes affecting life within the village.

Shortly before the last of the cottage smallholdings was given up, one of the longest held annual events in the village, that of the autumn livestock auction, fell by the wayside. This auction, first held in September 1880 on the plot of land adjoining the Exmoor Forest Hotel for the yeomen of the district, moved to the Barton in 1886, and there it continued for many years. The first Auctioneers were Messrs Gould and Sanders of Barnstaple, but at some time in the early 1920s, Cockram Dobbs and Stag took over, still using the site at the Barton. At a later date the auction was held in the field opposite Winstitchen Lane, and lastly in the field adjoining Little Crocombe.

With the demise of the small farmers in Simonsbath, who since the auction first began had been among its strongest supporters, and with other more profitable markets opening up, the Auctioneers decided to call it a day. The last of the stock auctions held in Simonsbath was in 1955, with just 750 sheep on offer, as against an average in earlier years of 1750 sheep and 75 bullocks. It is interesting to note that until the last few years, all the sheep on offer were of the Exmoor Horn Breed, and the cattle were all Devons, or Red Rubies as they are commonly known.

As one long established annual event began to die out, another took its place when in 1951 or 52 the first Exmoor Sheepdog Trials were held at Simonsbath, such trials having proved very popular in other parts of the Exmoor region. The first Simonsbath Trials was such a success it was decided to make it an annual event, and every year since it has been held on the first Friday in August.

At first, the Sheepdog Trials were held in the field above that on which the Round House or Shooting Tower stands. Early events held in this field were very much a social occasion, more like a fete, with stalls and draws for prizes etc. At a later date the Sheepdog Trials were held in the field adjoining Little Crocombe, but after a few years reverted to the original site.

Among those present at the first sheepdog trials was Jack Little—Mag's father—who was then nearly 80. He was accompanied by his granddaughter Shirley—Mag's youngest daughter—who at the time was no more than four or five years old. One spectator, Mrs Esther Thorne of Simonsbath Barton, was delighted to see the oldest and youngest members of the Little family there together. She told Mag it cheered her up no end.

Jack Little died a few years later in 1960, at the age of 86. He was the last of the second generation of the Little family shepherds on Exmoor. His father, William Little, was one of Frederic Knight's original Scottish shepherds, who came down to Exmoor in 1974, bringing a flock of sheep with him.

The proceeds from the first Sheepdog Trials at Simonsbath were given to the Lifeboat Station at Minehead, who showed their appreciation by inviting members of the committee, and others who had helped to raise funds, to come to Minehead, where they were all taken on a trip out to sea. Among those present were John Purchase—the Exmoor Estate Bailiff—and his wife; Frank and Nell Curtis, Bill Westacott, Will and Dor Little, Fred and Molly Land and one or two other estate shepherds.

One of the principle award winners at the Sheepdog Trials at Simonsbath was Fred Land, who for a time was a shepherd on the Exmoor Estate, and a National Sheepdog Trials Champion, who, according to a report in the *North Devon Journal* (11.8.1960), won all three awards that year; this being the fourth time he had won the Open at Simonsbath. Last year's winner, Jim Chapman of Stoke Pero—another former estate shepherd and winner of many awards—shared 4th place with Alf Little—Mag's brother. Alf, who is now in his late 70s, still competes. He too has won many cups and rosettes over the years, but sadly all were lost when the caravan in which he was living near Exford was destroyed by fire in July 1980.

There was a tragic accident in the village in January 1955, when George Clatworthy, who was married to the youngest of Dick Jones's daughters, Hilda, and for a short time lived in one of the cottages at Westgate, was killed while riding on—and operating—a council snowplough. It was so cold George lost his grip and fell in front of the plough, which passed over his body before it could be brought to a halt. At the time of his death he was living at Higher Thorne, Exford.

The centenary of the church of St Luke at Simonsbath was celebrated in October 1956. A number of services were held to mark the occasion, beginning with Holy Communion on Thursday 18th—St Lukes Day—and again on Friday morning. In the afternoon the church was crowded when the Bishop of Bath and Wells, the Rt. Rev. H.W. Bradley D.D. came there to preach. According to a report in the *West Somerset Free Press* (27.10.1956) all the parishioners who were able, seemed to be there, young and old. Among the latter were William Carter, John and George Thorne, Jack Little and William Prout, who as children were present when the Jubilee was celebrated in 1906, and judging by the number of young folk brought to the church on this occasion by their parents, it was anticipated that in 50 years time quite a few of them would be able to look back to the centenary occasion.

Among those present for Friday's service besides the Rev. W. B. Norris, Vicar of the parish of Exmoor, were the Rural Dean, the Rev. N. Owen; the Rev. R. A. W. Newman of Broomfield, former Rector of Withypool and Hawkridge; the Rev. P. D. Fox, Vicar of Winsford and Exton; the Rev. W. J. Prew, Vicar of North Molton and Twitchen, and the Rev. H. F. Warren of Exford.

Earl Fortescue was unable to attend but was represented by his Agent, Mr J. M. B. Mackie. Lady Fortescue sent some flowers to decorate the church. A big parish party was afterwards held in the Tea Room above the Exmoor Forest Hotel, with a grand tuck-in, to which all sat down; the Bishop cutting the huge 100 years birthday cake. It was indeed a day to be long remembered by the people of the parish of Exmoor.

On Saturday morning a Requiem was held in memory of the founders of the church and all departed benefactors and worshippers through the 100 years of its existence. Celebrations of the centenary were concluded on Sunday with Holy Communion in the morning and evensong, when the church was again well filled to hear the Rector of Hawkridge and Withypool, the Rev. P. P. Hopkinson, preach; the Rev. Norris taking the Service.

The death of Lord Fortescue—the 5th Earl—in June 1958, only four days after that of his wife, left the family without a direct heir as their only son Hugh Peter did not survive the Second World War. He was posted missing, presumed dead after the first battle at El Alamein in 1942. The title then passed on to the 5th Earl's brother, the Hon. Denzil Fortescue, but not the Castle Hill, Challacombe and Exmoor estates, which passed to the late Earl's eldest daughter, Lady Margaret—the wife of Bernard Van Cutsem, Esq.

The deaths of Lord and Lady Fortescue so close together, left the family with crippling death duties to pay, which necessitated the sale of a considerable portion of their landed estates, including the first sale of property to affect the Exmoor Estate since the 5th Earl inherited it in 1932.

The major sale of Fortescue Estate property in 1959 was preceded three years earlier on 7th Febrary 1956 by the sale of Simonsbath School, Schoolhouse, and adjoining White Rock Cottage, to the Somerset County Council Education Authority, who had been renting the school and schoolhouse since 1925. It was, perhaps, appropriate that what is believed to have been the first cottage built by John Knight in Simonsbath after he acquired the largest part of the former Royal Forest of Exmoor in 1818, should also be the first cottage in the village to be sold off.

When we last looked at the school, Miss Barralet was the headmistress, assisted by David Cripps, who taught the senior class in the old Meeting House. Miss Barralet gave up her post in 1951 and after a few months, when supply teachers filled the gap, Mrs Pye was appointed; her husband George finding employment on the estate.

Two years after Mrs Pye became headmistress, a school inspector called at the school. His report reveals that there were 20 pupils in attendance. All the boys were over the age of 11, and thus in the senior class; the girls were younger. The report also reveals there had been no improvements to the school since Miss Badger left some 15 years earlier. The water supply was still from a rainwater tank and a well on adjoining premises, and sanitary arrangements left much to be desired. It was understood the Education Authorities were about to remedy some of the defects.

The work of some of the senior pupils gave cause for concern, and the gardens were no longer cultivated. The senior boys were now travelling to

Dulverton one day each week for woodwork classes, physical education, and other specialist subjects, in which a keen interest was shown by all.

The school cook at this time was Dorothy (Dor) Little, who took up the post on the same day that her niece Shirley Prout started school (7.1.1952) and remained there until the school closed in 1970. Dor had so many relations attending the school it was not long before all the pupils were calling her Aunt Dor, and still do whenever they meet.

There was always plenty of work for the womenfolk of the village, particularly in the Exmoor Forest Hotel and the Lodge. At one time Dor was holding down three jobs at the same time, as well as looking after her family and a lodger.

One of Dor's earliest recollections as a small child living with her parents Dick and Sarah Jones at White Rock, was of being taken to North Molton to stay with her grandmother, Granny Prout, and of walking all the way home to Simonsbath afterwards with her granny, who knitted all the while as they went along. They stopped at the Poltimore Arms at Yarde Down for refreshments, and then continued on as before, with granny still knitting. By the time they reached Simonsbath, Dor—who could have been no more than seven or eight—was tired right out. Dor's mother was also a great knitter, and after the family moved to Cloven Rocks, she regularly knitted a sock in the time it took her to walk from the cottage to Simonsbath and back.

An application was made in 1952 to the Education Authority to instal Calor Gas lighting in the schoolroom in time for the winter evening classes, which had had to make do with old fashioned oil lamps. The request was turned down, and even after mains electricity was connected to the rest of the village in 1962, the authorities were still reluctant to connect it to the school, and it was only after pressure was brought to bear by the school managers that they relented and the decision was reversed.

In 1953, David Cripps was suspended from teaching for a short time while investigations were made into allegations that he had molested one of his pupils. The police quickly decided that there were no grounds whatsoever for a prosecution and the case was dropped. Nevertheless, Mrs Pye, the head-mistress, did not want him back; her complaint was that he would not co-operate with her and that his dress was very untidy for a teacher—a cardinal sin in those days. Notwithstanding her objections, David Cripps was re-instated, but shortly after, when pupil numbers had fallen to the stage where a second teacher was no longer required, he left to take up an appointment at Bampton.

When David Cripps first arrived on Exmoor in the early 1940s, the evacuee children were among his pupils. At that time he was lodging at Wintershead, but later moved in with Harry and Mag Prout, and more latterly still lodged with Amy Rich and her family at West Cottages.

While he was living in Simonsbath, David re-introduced cricket to the village after an absence of many years, and inter-village matches again became a regular summer pastime. The cricket pitch was on the 'splatt'

Jack Holman with Frank and Minnie Vigars, family and friends, to mark Frank's retirement after 33 years as the Simonsbath Post-master.

The Simonsbath and Exmoor Cricket Team.
(Back row) Harry Watts (Umpire), Ted Eaton, Henry Perry, Bill Winzer, Gordon Cheek, Bill Couch, (Front row) Gerald Eaton, Henry Prout, Fred Baker and daughter, Michael Vigars, Jack Watts.

Simonsbath Barton Farmhouse.

Hillcrest (Red Brick House).

above Rose Cottage, where childrens' and other sports were also held on a number of occasions.

By 1955, Mrs Pye too had left the village. her replacement was Mrs Neill, and as there had been no increase in pupil numbers attending the school, one classroom was found to be sufficient for their needs. The Meeting House was retained for a couple of years longer, just in case it was again needed as a classroom, but in October 1957, with news in the pipeline that Simonsbath School was to become a primary school only, it was given up. On 1st September in the following year, the village school became a primary school and thereafter, when pupils reached the age of 11, they were transferred to Dulverton Middle School, moving on to Minehead to finish their education.

There is little doubt that the change of status of Simonsbath School sealed its fate, and when Mrs Neill left in June 1960 there was grave concern in the village as to its future as numbers had again fallen, but by the time Mrs Beeson was appointed four months later, there were 14 children attending the school.

Mrs Beeson lasted less than three years, and a Miss Foxton was duly appointed to take her place. She was the last teacher at Simonsbath School, remaining there until it closed on 17th July 1970, at which time there were only three pupils. Dean Westlake was transferred to Dulverton Middle School, and Richard Smith and John Chapman to Exford Primary School. Pupil numbers had varied widely over the years at the Simonsbath school, and no doubt would have risen again, but despite a strong protest to this effect from the villagers, the school was closed down.

Since its closure, the school has been used as an activity centre by schools from away. It no longer belongs to the Somerset County Council, but is part of the County of Avon set-up.

On 18th September 1959, the whole of the Challacombe Estate of 5080 acres, along with 4643 acres of the Exmoor Estate, came under the hammer and was sold to a Crewkerne investment company. Within days both estates were in the hands of a Mr Spier, who in less than a fortnight split them up, selling the whole of the Exmoor section—which became known as the Emmetts Grange Estate—to a Mr Darby Haddon, a businessman from Gloucestershire.

The only property in Simonsbath included in this sale was the Exmoor Forest Hotel, along with about two acres of land adjoining, and the valuable rights of fishing on the River Barle, from—and including Pinkworthy Pond—downstream to a point a mile or so below Simonsbath. At this date the hotel was still in the tenancy of Mr H. J. Holman, who had taken a 7 year lease on the property in 1948, and a second lease in 1955 for 20 years, at a rental of £290 p.a.

At the time Mr and Mrs Holman moved into the hotel, social life in the village had become non-existent. The Saturday night social evenings, which throughout the war had been attended by 30-40 of the local inhabitants, had ceased soon after the war ended, and a monthly cinema show, started by Sir Robert Waley Cohen in a Nissen hut at Honeymead—where dances were also held—had likewise closed down after a run of three or four years.

The Nissen hut is well remembered by some of Simonsbath's older folk. It was beautifully done out inside and fitted with cinema-type seats. The hut was also used for a baby clinic. Mag has fond memories of a fancy dress competition held there, when she entered her very young son Henry as a shepherd, complete with a lamb she had made, and a shepherd's crook loaned for the occasion by Abe Antell, one of the estate shepherds; with Henry winning first prize.

Mr and Mrs Holman played a very active role in village life while they lived at the Exmoor Forest Hotel. He was a school manager for several years, and an ardent supporter of the Exmoor Foxhounds and numerous worthy local causes; organising whist drives etc. to raise funds. He also arranged for classic dance bands to come to the village, the dances being held in his Tea Room. It was not only the local inhabitants who turned up at these dances; folk from miles around came there to enjoy the music and dancing.

During the time Mr Holman was the tenant of the hotel, business again flourished, with Midland Red and Ribble coaches each making two regular calls a week throughout the summer months for lunch, which was served in the Tea Room. It was a busy time too in the hotel, with numerous guests coming and going. In the winter months, when it was quieter, Mrs Holman and Mag—who was now working at the hotel doing the cooking—used to make marmalade and chutney for the coming season. They did not have to worry too much about Mr Holman fussing about when they were making chutney, as he couldn't stand the smell of it being made and kept well away.

The winter of 1962/63, said to have been the worst in living memory, left Simonsbath cut off from the outside world for several weeks. During a short lull between blizzards in the middle of January 1963, the road from Exford to the village was cleared. This, according to a report in the *North Devon Journal* (17.1.63) enabled the ambulance service to bring Mrs Govier, the wife of George Govier—a shepherd living at Pinkery—and the latest addition to their family, from a Taunton hospital as far as Simonsbath, but no further, as the Challacombe road had not been cleared. Mrs Govier and her child were given overnight accommodation in the Vicarage by the wife of the vicar, the Rev. R. J. Fuller—the Rev. Norris's successor—and on the following day a helicopter arrived to airlift them home. This was the first time George had seen his three-week-old baby, as he had been unable to drive to Taunton because of the state of the roads. In the meantime he had been kept fully occupied looking after his flock of sheep and his other three children.

The lull between blizzards was soon over. The *North Devon Journal* (7.2.1963) reported all roads to Simonsbath again blocked with drifts up to 20ft deep on the Moor; reaching up to the roofs of farmhouses on the windward side.

With the roads blocked for so long, and with no bakery in the village, there were times when some of the inhabitants ran out of bread, so Mag, whose mother had always baked her own, set about baking bread in Mr and Mrs Holman's ovens at the Exmoor Forest Hotel. So good was the bread she made, her customers did not want her to stop when the crisis was over, but with guests arriving at the hotel, the ovens were required to supply their needs, so bread baking in the village came to an end.

One evening, when Will Little called at the hotel for his customary drink, Mr Holman told him that he had just put a lot of new fish in the river to improve the sport, but he was not worried about them as they were well protected from poachers by the local police and water bailiffs. Will later happened to mention this to one of his friends who said 'In that case we had better see what we can do about relieving him of a few'. Early the next morning Will's friend was out and about, returning home with a bowl-full of Mr Holman's new fish. He wouldn't have done it if Mr Holman had kept quiet about the matter. Poaching of one kind or another has always been rife on Exmoor. The Dulverton Petty Sessions Records are full of such prosecutions, including many by Frederic Knight when he owned the Exmoor and Brendon Estates.

In 1967, Mr Darby Haddon sold his Emmetts Grange Estate to Mr J. Bradley, retaining only the Exmoor Forest Hotel and fishing rights, which he gave to his daughter Celia, along with Lower House (Pound Cottages) and range of adjoining buildings, and the plot of land above the Exmoor Forest Hotel—where the new house now stands—which were not part of Mr Darby Haddon's original acquisition, but was conveyed to him on 24th December 1962.* By this time (1967) Mr and Mrs Holman had given up the hotel and a Mr and Mrs Pickmere had taken over the tenancy.

It was a sad day for Simonsbath when Mr and Mrs Holman left the village, particularly where its social activities were concerned. All dances, whist drives etc. ceased forthwith, and sadder still have never been resumed.

Mr and Mrs Pickmere believed the work in the hotel could be done with far fewer staff than had hitherto been employed by the Holmans, which quickly resulted in friction between management and employees. Too much was asked of the remaining staff; timetables could no longer be adhered to, and in consequence custom was lost, so Mag, who had stayed on as cook, decided to call it a day, handed in her notice and left.

Mr and Mrs Pickmere moved on in 1973. They were the last tenants of the Exmoor Forest Hotel. The next occupants, Mr and Mrs H. L. Sheldon, bought the hotel and fishing rights from Mr Darby Haddon's daughter, along with Lower House and the adjoining buildings.

During the three years or so that Mr and Mrs Sheldon owned the hotel it was managed by their son-in-law John Hall and their daughter Sonia, who, when the hotel and fishing rights were sold to Terry Woodward in 1976, bought Lower House and the range of buildings adjoining. By this time the property was in an almost derelict state. Little had been done to South Lower House during Harry Bond's last years, and nothing at all to North Lower House, which had lain empty since Harry's sister, Lucy Elworthy, moved out some years earlier. John Hall and his wife refurbished the two

* Information supplied by Mr Hugh Thomas

cottages into one unit, and Lower House reverted to its original name of Pound Cottage.

Two years or so after refurbishment, Pound Cottage and the adjoining buildings were sold to Rodney and Margaret Billington, who shortly after settling in, opened a pottery, and small shop on the premises to sell their wares, and other items. The pottery sold in the shop is made in Simonsbath but taken to another pottery they own at Blagborough on the Quantocks, for firing in the kiln there.

Terry Woodward was one of the longer term proprietors of the Exmoor Forest Hotel, and during his term of residence the business again prospered. Terry did much to regenerate and foster social activities in the village. He ran three skittle teams—Stags, Foresters and Abstainers; two darts teams and a pool team; without which, social life in Simonsbath would have been to all intents and purposes non-existent.

The Exmoor Forest Hotel was notable for another reason in Terry Woodward's day. He claimed—and probably with some justification—that he had the largest collection of different whiskies in the country, with 300 brand names on offer.

In 1989, Terry sold the hotel to Ian Frost and retired to Escott near Stogumber. Two years later the hotel again changed hands when Ian sold it to Trevor Impett, who, as a result of a rather unfortunate turn of events only a few months after his arrival, lost everything he possessed when the building society which had arranged his mortgage, crashed. The Exmoor Forest Hotel was then taken over by a bank, who placed it in the hands of Christies, the Auctioneers, to dispose of. While awaiting a buyer, Christies put in a manageress, who did her best in difficult circumstances to keep the hotel going, but by this time, with little money having been spent on maintenance in recent years, the hotel was badly in need of refurbishment.

The hotel was still in a sorry state when the present owner, Bob Sowden, bought it in 1992. He has spent a considerable sum of money on restoring it, and the hotel is now beginning to regain its rightful place in village life. I understand that Bob also plans to rebuild the Tea Room, which went out of use shortly before Terry Woodward retired; the floor of the building having become unsafe.

For many years, the annual church harvest supper and sale of harvest produce took place in the Tea Room. More recently this has been held in Boeveys Restaurant, but this year returned to the Exmoor Forest Hotel, where a splendid spread was put on.

When Postie Jones, the last of the cottage smallholders in the village, moved to Bridgwater in 1958, his cottage was assigned to Victor Charman, who had been taken on to the estate workforce as a mason and jack-of-all-trades. Shortly after, Den Westlake, a carpenter by trade, was also taken on; his base of operations being in the old sawmill.

Den's home in Simonsbath was in a newly created flat in John Knight's unfinished mansion, which had been reduced in size and roofed over shortly after Viscount Ebrington took over the Exmoor and Brendon Estates. The new flat, which became known as Diana Lodge Flat, was on the upper floor of the building; the ground floor remaining—as it had been for many years—a store.

Den, the first and only estate worker to live in this flat, continued to work on the estate until the time of his death 30 years later in December 1992, when he lost his courageous fight against cancer. Den's widow, Doreen, still lives in the flat by courtesy of the Fortescue famiy, who have always looked after their employees—their widows also—particularly those with long service records, who on retirement have either been allowed to remain in the cottage in which they had been living, or should this cottage be required for a service worker, found alternative accommodation in the village.

So it had been when Jim Little (Jack's brother) retired after a lifetime of service on the estate, first as a horseman and then for 40 years as a shepherd at Titchcombe, Toms Hill and Warren. Jim retired in 1950, and two years later moved into No. 4 West Cottages, which, since Eric Watts moved to Duredon in 1945, had been occupied by Bob Little—I,I'ys son—and then by Harry Couch, both of whom had worked on the estate for a time.

Sadly, Jim Little's stay at West Cottages was a short one. His wife died in 1954 and shortly after, he moved into a retirement home in Minehead.

At the time Jim Little left the village, Amy Rich and Leonard and Win Eaton were still living in the adjoining cottages. All were gone by 1958 and the three cottages empty, when, for the first time, they were let 'en bloc' to an outsider with no connection whatever with the estate. He was Flt. Lt. Copas, who was stationed at Chivenor. He moved into No. 4; his in-laws Mr and Mrs Dee into No. 5, and his son into No. 6. Mr Dee died while the family was living in the village and by 1963 the rest of the family had left Simonsbath.

As far as is known only No. 4 West Cottages was occupied thereafter while the cottages remained a part of the Exmoor Estate, the occupant—as already noted—being Will Hobbs and his wife, who lived there for about 6 years from 1963-1969.

All of the old block of West Cottages were again empty and in a near derelict state when they were sold off in 1972. According to Mr Hugh Thomas, the Fortescue Estate's Agent, the cottages were sold to Imogen Evans, a Vogue cover girl model, who was married to an architect, and though planning permission had been granted to demolish the cottages and rebuild, they were in fact restored and modernised. Shortly after this work was completed the cottages were sold off individually; all to people from away.

There were changes of occupants too at the Westgate Cottages. No. 1, originally designated as a service cottage for the use of the tenant of Simonsbath Barton, was—as already seen—the home of William Hunt and his wife from 1939 until his death in 1955, and it was from this base that William had run his smallholding. It may seem strange that George Thorne of the Barton should relinquish his one and only service cottage, but Alfie Smith, who succeeded William Webber as a general farm worker at the Barton, was a single man who lived in, and any other help that George required could be readily obtained in the village.

By the late 1950s, with less freely available labour to be had in the village, both of the cottages at Westgate were for a time occupied by men working at the Barton, Gerald Down, who lived in No. 1, and Gordon Coward in No. 2.

Gordon Coward is a descendant of one of the longest established families on Exmoor Proper. His ancestor, Robert Coward, was living in one of the Honeymead Cottages by 1844, but strangely, although members of this family had been living on Exmoor ever since, it was not until the late 1950s—or early 60s—that any of them took up residence in Simonsbath, and then it was not one, but two members of the family living there; Sid Coward being the other. Sid Coward was the son of Sid, who was Gordon's first cousin. He was living in No. 2 West Cottages in 1962, working on the estate, but in the following year, when Bill Batten and his wife left the village, Sid and his wife Phyllis moved to Jubilee Villas, where they remained until the early 1970s.

After a few years of working for George Thorne, Gordon Coward took over the village post round from Phyllis Prout, when she married Sante Lafuente—the head stockman living at Cornham—in 1965. Thereafter Gordon filled in his time and made up his wages by working as a jobbing labourer. He moved on to Ashott in the parish of Exford in or about 1970, but is believed to have continued to do the Simonsbath post round for a little longer, until—as already stated—the mail van driver took over.

Gerald Down—who had married one of Will Hobbs' daughters—continued to work for George Thorne until the latter retired in 1969 and moved to Exford, at which time both the Barton and the cottage in which he had been living, came in hand. Gerald then moved away from the village for a few years, but following Sante Lafuente's retirement, took his place at Cornham Farm.

Alfie Smith, who was also still working for George Thorne when he retired, moved with him to Exford. He later went to live with his sister at Yelland, and is believed to have ended his days at Swimbridge. He is remembered with affection by the older folk of Simonsbath, as a hard working dear old chap.

A year after the Barton was taken in hand, Duredon, the last of the tenanted farms on the Exmoor Estate, also came in hand when Eric Watts, who had been associated with the farm for 50 years, first working for his father-in-law William Elworthy and then on his own account, retired and went to Clatworthy to live near his married daughter. With his retirement another long established custom, that of the Rent Audit, held twice yearly in the Estate Office and adjoining Reading Room, also died out, as the little land and property still let did not warrant a Rent Audit. In former days, when Frederic Knight was the owner of the Exmoor and Brendon Estates, his Rent Audits were held at Red Deer (Gallon House).

John Hayes, the Exmoor Estate Bailiff since 1953, died in 1970. It was then decided that future bailiffs—or Under Managers as they were now known—should live at the Barton, and Hillcrest (Red Brick House) was sold off.

Hillcrest, advertised in the *North Devon Journal* in September 1970, was described as a well modernised 4 bedroom house. Included in the sale were two looseboxes and a range of other useful outhouses, a garden and a pasture paddock, amounting to about 3 acres in all.

The property was bought by Mr and Mrs Johns, who were hunting people. Two years or so later they sold it to Mrs Chown's father, Mrs Chown being the present owner.

For a short time, when Mrs Chown's husband was Bailiff on the Exmoor Estate (having succeeded Douglas Batchelor and John Ault—John Hayes' successors), they lived at the Barton, before moving on to Hillcrest; mainly because Mrs Chown, a keen horsewoman, found Hillcrest to be a more suitable place to keep her horses, and though she and her husband have long since parted and he has moved on, Mrs Chown continued to live at Hillcrest, and still does.

After Simonsbath Barton came in hand, the farmhouse was divided into two cottages; the other cottage there providing accommodation for a general farm worker. According to Frank Vigars, one part of the farmhouse appears to be much older than the other, and judging by the number of outside doors, he believes the house could well have been in divided occupation at an earlier date, which is not unlikely when we consider that other cottages in the village, smaller than the farmhouse at the Barton, were at times occupied by two or more families.

It was at this time that a new range of farm buildings were erected at the Barton and another set of buildings constructed east of the Brendon Road, opposite the top lane into the farm. Thirteen loads of ready-mix concrete, which had been rejected by the Ministry of Transport constructing the M5 motorway, arrived one day, which was used to make up the lane into the Barton, and to the other new farm buldings. Rejected the concrete may have been, but it has survived better than that appoved by the Ministry which was used on the motorway, much of which has since been dug up and renewed.

It was around this time too that Viscount Ebrington's stables adjoining Rose Cottage were demolished and a tractor house built in their stead. The coach house was left as it was. For some years past it had been used to store fertilizer, and for a time after mains electricity was connected to the village, it was used for shearing the sheep from the Limecombe and Ashcombe herdings; the sheep being housed overnight prior to shearing in the stables next door, but since the new buildings were erected at the Barton they have been sheared there.

For a short time after Major Cooke and his family left the village, Simonsbath Lodge was without an occupant. It had been intended by the Fortescue Estate that Mr Hugh Thomas, their Agent, should live there, but as Mrs Thomas was following a career as a teacher this was not convenient, so for a time they remained where they were at Castle Hill, later moving into the family home at Bishops Tawton.

On looking around the old house at Simonsbath, Mr Thomas was rather surprised to find the matchboard partitions in a passageway upstairs painted mauve and yellow on alternate boards, particularly so seeing as how the last tenant, Major Cooke, was such a dedicated conservationist. In fact, there is no evidence that Major Cooke was responsible for this act of vandalism; the painting could well have been done at an earlier date, possibly when the house was used as a school.

After Mr Thomas declined the offer to move into Simonsbath Lodge it was decided to sell the property. It was then divided into three lots, with the estate retaining only that part of the property where Den Westlake was living with his family; namely John Knight's unfinished mansion building.

Lot 1, which was called Forest Lodge, consisted of the east wing of the old house, and a plot of land adjoining to the east above the old road to the Lodge from the Exmoor Forest Hotel end. There was once a large building on this plot of land, near the house, but no one I have spoken to can remember it or what it was used for.

Lost 2, Simonsbath Lodge, was the whole of the central part of the old house, and the forecourt and grounds extending southwards to the main road and eastwards as far as Ashcombe Water. This lot also included the old cart linhay, Estate Office and Reading Room, along with about half of the courtyard outside.

Lot 3, Diana Lodge, was comprised of the newer west wing of the house, also the Racquets Court and the old Wool Chamber, together with the other half of the cart linhay courtyard.

Lots 2 and 3 were acquired by John Morley and his girlfriend and business partner Jeanette Fay, to whom both properties were conveyed on the 25.3.1969. They also took a 21-year-lease on Lot 1 at a rental of £156 p.a., with the object of purchasing it later.*

John and Jeanette then set about the task of turning the old house into a proper hotel, and to this end the old kitchen was enlarged by extending it outwards at the back of the house. The old Racquets—or Squash—court, long disused, was also restored and people from near and far came to play there.

Shortly after John Morley and Jeanette Fay took possession of the old house, which became known as the Simonsbath House Hotel, a new Post Office and shop was opened up in the west wing, to replace the Post Office and Stores at Jubilee Villas, which had now closed down; John and Brenda Watts having moved to Bratton Fleming. A year later they returned to the village, with John back in his old job as a tractor driver and general farm worker on the estate farm. They took up residence in No. 1 Westgate Cottages, which had come in hand with the Barton, and have remained there ever since, with John still working on the estate.

At the time John Morley and Jeanette Fay took over their Simonsbath property—and for some time after—they lived in London during the week, as both had highly paid jobs there; only coming down to Simonsbath at weekends. The day-to-day running of the hotel was left in the hands of a manager, who ran the business with the help of local and other staff. The Post Office and shop were looked after by Millie Curtis—Stan's wife—for three or four years. She also did the cooking.

* Information supplied by Mr Hugh Thomas

Mag, who had given up her job at the Exmoor Forest Hotel, was in the Post Office one day when Millie asked her if she would be interested in doing some of the cleaning work in the hotel, as they were looking for a cleaner. Mag took the job, and later took over much of the cooking as well.

Although the old house cannot be said to be haunted, two young girls from Manchester, who were working there and living in, became convinced that it was, having heard footsteps up and down the passageway outside their room late at night. Human nature being what it is, this was played on by villagers working in the hotel, to the extent that the girls refused to sleep in the room again and John Morley was forced to give them alternative accommodation. The 'ghostly' footsteps were in fact those of John Morley's son—who was given to wandering about the hotel in the middle of the night. Nevertheless, two visitors who called at the hotel one day for a cream tea, who were given a tour of the old house by John Morley, after telling him they were very interested in old houses and any associated psychic phenomena, detected a 'presence' of some kind in three of the bedrooms there; two in the older part of the house, the other in the newer west wing. Mag tells me that her youngest daughter Shirley, and a later girlfriend of John Morley, never felt comfortable in the latter bedroom. Shirley said it gave her the creeps.

There is a story handed down through successive generations of old Simonsbath and Exmoor families, which may or may not account for the 'presence' found by the two visitors in one of the older bedrooms. The story I have heard concerns the untimely death of Frederic Knight's son— also Frederic—in 1879, which was not, it is alleged, from natural causes, but in more mysterious circumstances. Suffice to say here, it did not go down well in the close-knit Knight family circle when they learned that young Frederic was paying court to one of the local girls—a commoner—and wished to marry her. The girl is said to have been one of the daughters of William Scott—the Exmoor Estate Bailiff—who, Jack Buckingham told me, was one of two daughters who in fact never married. What is known for certain is that within a very short time of William Scott's death in 1875, all of the family, most of whom were in service employment on the estate, were gone from Exmoor, though not—it is believed—very far away, as both of William Scott's unmarried daughters were later buried in the churchyard at Simonsbath.

On one of his journeys back to London after spending a weekend at Simonsbath, John Morley was seriously injured in a car crash near Wylye in Wiltshire; his business partner and girlfriend Jeanette Fay, who was with him, was killed in the accident. John spent several months in Salisbury Hospital before he was well enough to pick up the threads of his life once more.

On his retirement from his well paid job in London, John Morley commuted a large part of his pension into cash in order to complete the purchase of the Simonsbath House Hotel; the last part, Forest Lodge—Lot 1—being conveyed to him on the 7th May 1973. In the following year he took an option on part of Ashcombe Plantation, this being part of the former pleasure grounds of the old house.*

John Morley never took up his option. He told Stan Curtis that in order to complete his purchase of the hotel he had commuted too large a portion of his pension, which left him with very little to live on, and he was thus unable to complete his refurbishment plans for the old house. Shortly after, John sold the hotel to Malcolm Wood and his wife Janet, who bought it with a little help from Malcolm's mother. Mrs Wood senior took up the option on the former pleasure grounds of the house, purchasing them in her own right.

Malcolm Wood and his family were still living at the Simonsbath House Hotel when the village was once again cut off from the outside world by huge snowdrifts in the winter of 1978. A helicopter was used to bring in supplies, as it had been in the winter of 1962/63. At that time food had been distributed free of any charges, and human nature being what it is, this had been taken advantage of by some of the Simonsbath residents, who in fact were not short of supplies, and assuming the same rules would apply when the helicopter landed in the village on this occasion, one or two villagers arrived at the Simonsbath House Hotel to collect another free hand-out, but on hearing from Malcolm Wood—who was handling the distribution—that all goods had to be paid for at market prices, one of the villagers, half muttering to herself, said she didn't really need anything and returned home empty handed.

In 1979, Malcolm Wood sold the hotel to Mr and Mrs Archie Brown, who continued the task of restoring the property, and at the same time gained a high reputation for the excellence of their cuisine, but after five years they too moved on, selling the property to the present owners, Mike and Sue Burns.

Mag, who had continued working at the hotel after John Morley gave it up—first for Malcolm and Janet Wood, and then for the Browns—retired at the age of 74, two years before Mike and Sue took over the property; her health at that time giving cause for concern.

In the eight years that Mike and Sue have been the proprietors of the Simonsbath House Hotel, many further improvements have been made to the property, all of which have been carried out to a very high standard, whilst retaining the character of the place; Mike being a former architect by profession. For the sake of posterity I would now like to record the alterations and additions to the property carried out by Mike, and those of earlier years, apart from that done by Viscount Ebrington around the turn of the century, and minor alterations when Major Cooke was living there, which have already been noted.

During work carried out to the roof of the tower above the main entrance to the hotel, Mike discovered that the tower originally had a parapet, which must have leaked, because a new roof had been constructed at some time

* Information supplied by Mr Hugh Thomas

using the parapet as a base. This roof has been renewed by Mike. He believes the original principle entrance to the house was on the line of the main building, inside the tower, though the tower itself is undoubtedly very old. Mike believes too that the original house consisted of just three rooms on the ground floor; that the building was no more than 18ft wide, and that there was no east wing, though this wing (later used as a caretaker's quarters) is also believed to be of early date judging from its construction and old beams revealed during recent work done to the ceiling. Mike has left the beams exposed, adding much to the character of this room. He has also cleared out the cellar of the house—part of the original building—which was full of rubble.

According to Mag, the rubble was tipped into the cellar by Archie Brown when he exposed the main fireplace of the old house, above which is the dated beam of 1654. Three fireplaces were removed to get to the original, one of which was Victorian. The entrance to the cellar, which adjoins the fireplace, was no doubt considered a useful place to tip the rubble, as Archie Brown no longer had any use for it.

When Mag first came to know the old house, a large black Bodley stove stood in front of the old fireplace. This was later replaced with a Rayburn.

The cellar of the house is interesting, stone steps leading down to a large room, the floor of which is covered by large stone slabs, which around the walls have been raised to a higher level to take barrels of ale etc; many gallons of which were brewed on the premises in earlier years. This was not the only cellar to the original house; the other, adjoining to the east, was filled in when Viscount Ebrington lowered the floor of the room above. Mag tells me that when John Morley's workmen were excavating at the rear of the house for the extension of his kitchen, an arched blocked-up doorway, below ground level at that time—beneath one of the ground floor windows— was discovered.

Access to the east wing of the house, for many years the caretaker's and servants' quarters, is, as would be expected, from inside the main building. Presumably it was always so, but there was once a somewhat peculiar arrangement in regards to another access to these rooms—on the first floor—where by removing the partition at the back of a large cupboard it was possible to gain an entry at this level. On reflection, it hardly seems likely that access at this level was always so complicated. If, as suspected, it was Viscount Ebrington who had this cupboard made—which in living memory has always been used as an airing cupboard—why did he bother to have an easily removable partition put in at the back of cupboard, when it would have been far more sensible to seal off this entrance completely.

While stripping off the old plaster on the front wall of the house preparatory to replastering, Mike Burns discovered there had once been another window along this wall, which was situated at the east end of the original building, between two other windows at a point where the downpipe from the rainwater guttering is now fixed.

Before we leave the old house, one more item remains to be recorded. This concerns Lord Fortescue's personal toilet, a fine example of wrought ironwork, which, according to Mag, was removed by John Morley on the understanding it would be preserved. I would be most interested to learn what became of it.

In the last two or three years, Mike and Sue have converted the old Wool Chamber into three holiday flats, and turned the old cart linhay into Boevey's Restaurant, both of which have proved very popular, and, having now achieved all they set out to do, are thinking of moving on to a fresh challenge. They will be missed in the village, where they have become very much a part of the community.

The church too has seen changes in recent years. The amalgamation of the parishes of Exmoor and Exford under one vicar, first sought by Lord Fortescue in the mid-1940s, finally came about in 1975,[2] the first vicar of the combined parishes being the Rev. Box, who took up residence in the Vicarage at Exford. Since that date the parishes of Hawkridge and Withypool have been added to the vicar's domain. In the same year that the Rev. Box took over the Exmoor and Exford livings, the Vicarage at Simonsbath was sold to Mr and Mrs Du Parc Braham. It has recently again changed hands.

Shortly before the Rev. Box took over the parishes of Exmoor and Exford, the outgoing vicar of Exford, the Rev. Warren, had the notion to find someone within the parish of Exmoor to play the organ in St Lukes Church on a regular basis for the new vicar; the organist of late having been non-resident. Mag's name was put forward by one of the parishioners, and the Rev. Warren duly called around to see her and asked her if she would take the job, but Mag, who had not played the organ since the departure of the Rev. Norris, declined to do so, whereupon the vicar said, 'I am very disappointed in you Mrs Prout, I would have thought you would have done your bit for the church!' Mag's response was that as she had played the organ in the church for 11 years and been on the Church Council for 33 years, as well as cleaning the church for some of them, she considered she had done her bit. The vicar went off in a huff and never spoke to her again.

There have been further sales of property in and around Simonsbath in the last 20 years, all of which was—or had formerly been—part of the Exmoor Estate.

On 29th August 1973, Birch Cleave Wood, extending to about 26½ acres, was sold to the Somerset County Council and vested in the Exmoor National Park Authority; this being the first land in Simonsbath to pass into their hands. Mr Hugh Thomas informs me that if he remembers correctly, the estate had proposed to fell the wood, much of which had reached—or passed—maturity, and then to replant with beech and a nurse crop of conifers. The licence to fell was refused on the grounds that it was the highest beech wood—or one of the highest—in the country. Ironically, after acquiring the wood, the National Park Authority became aware that when trees are past their prime they do decay and become dangerous, and much of the wood has now been felled and replanted with beech and conifers, in

Boevey's Restaurant and Rose Cottage.

*Stable Flat and rear view of Simonsbath House Hotel, with part of
John Knight's kennels (left of foreground).*

Stable Flat, former Estate Office, Reading Room and Boevey's Restaurant, with the old Woolchamber (Flats) behind.

Simonsbath Saw Mill and associated buildings.

much the same way as was proposed by the estate when they applied for a felling licence.

Five years after the Somerset County Council acquired Birch Cleave Wood, they made their second purchase of land in Simonsbath, when they bought all that part of Ashcombe Plantation that Mrs Wood senior had bought shortly after her son and daughter-in-law acquired the Simonsbath House Hotel. The new acquisition by the County Council was also placed in the care of the National Park Authority, who have since made a car park in part of the grounds, and converted the old Higher Stables into toilets and a store. Also included with their purchase was the old Gospel Hall—Meeting House—site, which was afterwards sold to Ron Smith, who had a house built there. The only reminder that this was once the site of the Gospel Hall is to be found in the School Lane outside, where two pillars mark the former entrance to the hall.

The next property to change hands in the village was the old range of farm buildings on the east side of the road opposite the Exmoor Forest Hotel, which the estate sold to David Little in January 1982. David, son of Will and Dor Little, has started work on converting the buildings into a dwelling house, and intends one day to return to Simonsbath to live there.

Only two other dwelling houses have been built in—or close to—the village. One, a bungalow, was erected on a site acquired by Kempton Jones from the Honeymead Estate, which was situated in the corner east of Winstitchen Lane, adjacent to the Simonsbath-Exford road. For 12 years after Harry Watts' death, Kempton—a descendant of Eli Jones—provided the Simonsbath School car service, until it closed in 1970. In more recent years he has provided a local taxi service. Kempton's bungalow goes under the name of White Rocks, which should not be confused with the much older property in the village, the name of which disappeared when the Somerset County Counil acquired it along with the school and schoolhouse. Kempton's bungalow, which has been on the market for some time, has now been sold, and another long-familiar figure around the village has moved on.

Of the latest house built in the village, the less said the better. Although a pleasant enough house in the right setting, it can hardly be said to be in character with the rest of the village, especially where it is sited on such a prominent position beside the main road above the Exmoor Forest Hotel. This plot, for many years part of the grounds of the hotel, was sold by Ian Frost to Brian Ward, a builder from Heasley Mill. It is hard to understand how planning permission was granted in the first place for such a house, when far more worthy applications, in less obtrusive positions, have been turned down by the National Park Planning Authority; particularly so in this instance when there was no local demand for it as there were already several empty cottages in the village. The new house has now stood there without an occupant for more than two years, and in the present economic climate looks likely to continue to.

On 9th September 1991, all of the remaining open moorlands belonging to the Exmoor Estate, amounting to about 4200 acres, was conveyed to the

Somerset County Council and placed in the safe keeping of the National Park Authority for present and future generations to enjoy. This acquisition included Burcombe, Halscombe and some better land on Mount Pleasant adjoining; a large part of the old Deer Park and Great Woolcombe; in fact, all of the remaining estate lands south of the River Barle changed hands, along with the river meadows below Simonsbath Bridge. Moorlands on the northern part of the Exmoor Estate, including Exe Plain, Great and Little Buscombe, and Lanacombe, also passed to the National Park Authority.*

On the terms of the agreement, the Exmoor Estate have a 40 year non-exclusive grazing right on their former moorlands, which in effect has drastically reduced the amount of stock they can depasture there, as a direct result of which the number of sheep herdings on the estate have been reduced from five to three. The number of breeding ewes in each of the remaining herdings has been increased from about 830 to 1000. Shearing is done by contract, but it is left to the three shepherds to find their own help at lambing time.

The number of tractor drivers cum general farm workers has likewise been reduced to three since Stan Curtis retired and was not replaced. A stockman and an assistant stockman-general farm worker make up the full time staff on the estate farm. Two former full time emplyees, now semi-retired, work two and a half days a week repairing fences, dry stone walls etc. Accommodation is provided rent free and craftsman's rates are paid, perks include wood and peat for fuel, but only Sante Lafuente, John Watts and Peter Charman still dig the latter. Their turf pits are on Buscombe.[3] A non-contributary pension scheme, introduced many years ago, has also proved its worth, and has been of great benefit to long service employees on their retirement.

The estate farm, now reduced to less than 2500 acres, has been run from Castle Hill by the Fortescue Estates Farm Manager Ron Smith for the past seven years. The former Under Manager's house at Simonsbath Barton is currently occupied by Mark Oddy—Mr Thomas's assistant—but as his duties concerning the Exmoor Estate now take up only one day a week, most of his time is spent at Molland, where he is more gainfully employed on the Molland Estate.

The death of Den Westlake, and the retirement of Victor Charman, who moved down to Filleigh, has left the village without a resident carpenter and mason for the first time since John Knight laid down the foundations of the village in—or about—the year 1820, as neither have been replaced. Maintenance and other repair work is now either carried out by tradesmen from the Castle Hill Estate, or done by local building firms. Large jobs on the estate farm, such as silage making, is now a joint operation with the help of tractor drivers and machinery from Castle Hill; the Simonsbath men in their turn helping out at Filleigh.

Thus we find only five full time and two part-time estate employees living

---

* Information supplied by Mr Hugh Thomas

in the village as defined within the boundaries of Limecombe at Westgate, and that of Winstitchen Lane, with three more living outside these boundaries; a stockman at Cornham Farm, and shepherds at Cornham Bungalow and Black Pits.

Of the other cottages in the village still owned by the Exmoor Estate, three are lived in by retired employees or their widows, and a further four are let to people from neighbouring villages; the two Council Houses likewise, although the father of one of the tenants did work on the estate as a shepherd for a few years.

Nine dwelling houses, including the Vicarage, are now in private hands. One more awaits a buyer, and another is in the course of conversion from old farm buildings. The two hotels and three holiday flats complete the picture of Simonsbath as it is today.

One further change of ownership of property in Simonsbath is in the pipeline. The Exmoor National Park Authority has an option to buy the sawmill premises, which have not been used since the death of Den Westlake. It seems likely they will take up the option as the lease of their present premises at Yenworthy is running out. With all of the machinery in the Simonsbath sawmill in good working order, this could prove to be a wise long term investment. There is talk too—should the option be taken up—of the leat to the mill being cleaned out and the turbine brought back into use on special occasions for public demonstrations. I have fond memories of the sawmill, because it was here that I first met the late Jack Buckingham and our friendship was forged.

Despite the growth of Simonsbath over the years, the social life of the village is at a very low ebb. Darts, skittles and pool are still played at the Exmoor Forest Hotel, but other social activities have been reduced to the annual Sheepdog Trials; and for a few years past, a Fun Day, which more recently still has included a Duck Race. This event is held in the river meadow below Simonsbath Bridge. The proceeds provide an annual Christmas party for the children of the parish.

Inevitable as some of the changes over the last 50 years have been, Simonsbath today has joined the ranks of other villages on and around the Moor, where people from away outnumber the local inhabitants.

There is now only one person left in Simonsbath who was living there at the time of the First World War. That person is Margaret (Mag) Prout of Rose Cottage, a very dear friend to my wife and myself. Mag, and a rapidly declining number of former Simonsbath folk now living in villages around the Moor—all of whom are either in their eighties, or fast approaching them—are the last surviving witnesses of life in Simonsbath as it was in the old days, when for generation after generation sons followed their fathers on to the estate, or took over the cottage smallholdings. In the course of time these old Exmoor families inter-married, and for many years it was hard to find anyone in the village who was not related, making it a very close-knit community indeed.

The oldest surviving members of this close-knit community have also witnessed the gradual disintegration of the Exmoor Estate, as bit by bit has been sold off. This, coupled with increased mechanisation on the estate farm in more recent years has taken a further toll on the old families, many members of which have also moved on. Question those who remember Simonsbath in the old days, as to whether they preferred the village as it used to be, or as it is now with every modern convenience—washing machines, television, cars etc; and without hesitation, all will plump for the old days, despite their deprivations.

The more recent employees taken on by the Exmoor Estate do not have the same feeling for the village and its past history, nor is there any reason why they should; their roots did not flourish in the Exmoor soil.

As this century draws to a close, so too does the end of another era, as sadly, one by one, the small band of Simonsbath stalwarts diminishes year by year, taking their memories with them. All too soon they will all be gone, and the village that I have come to love and know so well, will have lost much of its fascination, and not a little of its character and charm.

NOTES

CHAPTER 5

Page 43   1   Although Henry Scale was only employed by Dowlas as Mining Superintendent of their operations on Exmoor from 1856-58, Henry and his family remained on the moor for at least two more years, during which time a daughter, Joanne, died (12th April 1859), at the age of only 18, and Henry's wife, Sarah Ann (2nd January 1860), at the age of 49. Both were buried in the Simonsbath churchyard.

           The Rev. Thornton, in his reminiscences, remarks that Henry Scale, a deeply religious man, tried to revive his daughter on her deathbed by annointing her with oil and calling upon her to rise up and walk.

Page 48   2   An undated letter from Lady Knight at Wolverley to George Molland, the Exmoor Estate Bailiff, reveals that she had received a sad letter from old Fry (William), telling her he had been turned out by his son (Charles) who was in arrears with his rent, and not for the first time. Lady Knight was most upset when she learned of what had been done to the old father, and though she had forgiven Charles Fry some back rent that was due at the last Rent Audit, she was adamant she would not give up the rent again, and asked George Molland for his advice on how to act.

CHAPTER 7

Page 79   1   In March 1920, a Captain Mills, who had taken Honeymead House as a hunting box, was on his way to a meet when he was thrown from his horse and killed. The spot where he met his death was on the Brendon road, just above the top entrance to Simonsbath Barton and very close to where the body of Harriet Mabel Willand was found. Was it a coincidence, or was his horse 'spooked' by her ghost?

CHAPTER 8

Page 96   1   After losing his job on the post-round, Frank Vigars set up a car hire business; he doing the driving. He later bought a tractor and did contract work, but the WarAg mucked him about so much he decided to call it a day. He then moved to Honeymead with his wife Olive (daughter of William Watts) and for the next 38 years until his retirement worked as a jack-of-all-trades for the Waley-Cohen family.

CHAPTER 8 (contd.)

Page 108   2 The first regular milk delivery service in the village was carried out by Mr J.F. A'Brooke of Ludslade, Exford who was allowed to rent some of the Lower House land from the Exmoor Estate in 1953, on condition that he supplied the village with milk. He was followed by Mr Robert Smith of Luckwell Bridge, who also delivered the newspapers and then by Minehead Dairies, who do likewise, though the postman does deliver some newspapers.

CHAPTER 9

Page 115   1 Lady Margaret Fortescue tells me that although mains electricity was connected to the village in 1962, the estate still provides everybody in Simonsbath with free water as they have been unable to persuade South West Water to install a mains supply.

Page 132   2 In fact there was already a form of amalgamation before this date, as the Rev. Fuller, vicar of Exmoor, residing at Simonsbath Vicarage, was also vicar of the parish of Challacombe.

Page 134   3 Mr Hugh Thomas informs me that when the Fortescue Estates sold the last of their moorlands on Exmoor to the Exmoor National Park Authority in 1991, it was agreed that the villagers should continue to enjoy their customary privilege of digging peat.

BIBLIOGRAPHY

Acland Archive—DRO Exeter.

Billingsley, John—*General View of the Agriculture of Somerset 1795*

Census Returns of Exmoor and the Bordering Parishes

Electoral Rolls for Exmoor

Exeter Flying Post

Exmoor Review—various.

Fortescue Archive—DRO Exeter and Castle Hill Estate Office.

Kelly's Directories of Somerset.

Knight Archive—Kidderminster Reference Library.

MacDermot E. T. and R. J. Sellick—*The History of the Forest of Exmoor 1970.*

North Devon Journal.

Orwin C. S. and R. J. Sellick—*The Reclamation of Exmoor Forest, 1970.*

Parish Registers—Exmoor and the Bordering Parishes.

Sherborne Mercury.

Smith-Richards G. C. Diaries—Fortescue Archive DRO Exeter.

Taunton Courier.

Thornton, Rev. W. H.—*Reminiscences and Reflections of an Old Westcountry Clergyman,* Vols I and II 1897

West Somerset Free Press.

Other sources of information as stated in the text.

INDEX